ポンポン話すための瞬間英作文パターン・プラクティス

反射的に言える

森沢洋介 =著

Emily is in her room.
Emily was in her room an hour ago.
Emily will be in New York tomorrow.
Will you be in New York tomorrow?

はじめに

　英語を自由に話すには、基本文型を自在に駆使できなければなりません。簡単な英文をスピーディーに、たくさん作る瞬間英作文トレーニングは、基本文型を反射的に使いこなす能力を身につけるために、非常に効果的です。

とは言え、初級から中級レベルの学習者が連続的に英文を作り出すことを、自力で行っていくのは困難です。目に見えること、心に浮かぶことを英語にしようとしても、表現の仕方に迷い、練習が進まず、たくさんの文を作るということにたちまち挫折してしまいます。そこで、英文を作り出すための引き金が必要となります。本書に先立つ、「どんどん話すための瞬間英作文トレーニング」「スラスラ話すための瞬間英作文シャッフルトレーニング」では、簡単な日本語の短文を引き金として使いました。

　本書では新たに、元の文を少しずつ変えていくという方法を導入します。パターン・プラクティスと呼ばれるものです。この方法では、英文を作るために、独立した文の代わりに、主に、単語、フレーズを、新しい文を作るきっかけとして使います。

　日本語文を丸ごと使うと、日本語の意味の咀嚼やイメージ化に困

難を感じたり、日本語に振り回され、英作文というより英文の暗記になってしまう方が少なからずいます。本書のパターン・プラクティスだと、日本語の使用が最小限なので、このような問題が起こりにくくなります。また、文を一時的に記憶する負担がなくなるので、トレーニングの負荷は非常に軽く、その結果スピード感が増すことになります。

　実は、パターン・プラクティスは、数十年前に盛んに使われたメソッドですが、現在ではあまり日が当たることがありません。世の中の他のジャンルと同じで、外国語教育の理論、手法にも、流行り廃りがあるのは致し方ありません。若い人の間では、パターン・プラクティスという言葉さえ聞いたことがない方が多いでしょう。しかし、基礎レベルにいる人に必ず効果をもたらしてくれるメソッドです。「古くて新しい」このメソッドを用い、新たな角度から、新たな刺激で、瞬間英作文トレーニングを行ってみてください。

ポンポン話すための瞬間英作文 パターン・プラクティス●もくじ

はじめに 3

本書の特長 10
本書の構成とステージ進行における位置づけ 17
本書の使い方 20
本書でトレーニングする上での注意点 24
瞬間英作文 パターン・プラクティスのやり方 26

基礎編 29

❶快速トレーニング① 30
❷快速トレーニング② 32
❸快速トレーニング③ 34
❹快速トレーニング④ 36
❺快速トレーニング⑤ 38
❻快速トレーニング⑥ 40
❼快速トレーニング⑦ 42
❽快速トレーニング⑧ 44
❾快速トレーニング⑨ 46
❿快速トレーニング⑩ 48
⓫快速トレーニング⑪ 50

⑫快速トレーニング⑫　52
⑬快速トレーニング⑬　54
⑭快速トレーニング⑭　56
⑮快速トレーニング⑮　58
⑯快速トレーニング⑯　60
⑰現在完了―1 完了　62
⑱現在完了―2 継続　64
⑲現在完了―3 経験　66
⑳快速トレーニング⑰　68
㉑快速トレーニング⑱　70
㉒快速トレーニング⑲　72
㉓快速トレーニング⑳　74
㉔快速トレーニング㉑　76
㉕快速トレーニング㉒　78
㉖快速トレーニング㉓　80
㉗快速トレーニング㉔　82
㉘快速トレーニング㉕　84
㉙快速トレーニング㉖　86
㉚快速トレーニング㉗　88
㉛快速トレーニング㉘　90
㉜快速トレーニング㉙　92
㉝快速トレーニング㉚　94
㉞快速トレーニング㉛　96
㉟快速トレーニング㉜　98

㊱快速トレーニング㉝　100
㊲快速トレーニング㉞　102
㊳快速トレーニング㉟　104
㊴快速トレーニング㊱　106
㊵快速トレーニング㊲　108
㊶快速トレーニング㊳　110

発展編　113

❶受動態―1　114
❷受動態―2　116
❸受動態―3　118
❹受動態―4　120
❺must、can't、may　122
❻have to、be going to、be able to　124
❼不定詞―1 名詞的用法　126
❽不定詞―2 形容詞的用法　128
❾不定詞―3 副詞的用法（目的）　130
❿不定詞―4 副詞的用法（感情の原因）　132
⓫動名詞―1 目的語　134
⓬動名詞―2 主語　136
⓭比較―1　138
⓮比較―2　140

⑮SVO＋to 不定詞—1 want　142
⑯SVO＋to 不定詞—2 ask　144
⑰SVO＋to 不定詞—3 tell　146
⑱that 節—1　148
⑲that 節—2　150
⑳間接疑問文—1　152
㉑間接疑問文—2　154
㉒従属節—1　156
㉓従属節—2　158
㉔分詞—1　160
㉕分詞—2　162
㉖関係代名詞—1（文から関係代名詞節への変換—1）　164
㉗関係代名詞—2（文から関係代名詞節への変換—2）　166
㉘関係代名詞—3　168
㉙関係代名詞—4　170
㉚関係代名詞—5　172
㉛原形不定詞—知覚動詞1　174
㉜原形不定詞—知覚動詞2　176
㉝原形不定詞—使役動詞1　178
㉞原形不定詞—使役動詞2　180

本書の特長

　瞬間英作文トレーニングは、簡単な英文を大量に作ることで、英文を頭の中で考え込むことなく、スピーディーに作る能力、つまり**瞬間英作文回路**を作ることを目的とします。「どんどん話すための瞬間英作文トレーニング」「スラスラ話すための瞬間英作文シャッフルトレーニング」に続く瞬間英作文テキストである本書では、主に**パターン・プラクティス**の手法によるトレーニングを行います。パターン・プラクティスとは引き金になるセンテンスの一部（主語や目的語など）を変えたり、時制や態を変換するなどして、無数の文を作り出していく練習です。

　例えば、練習する人が

I go to the library every day.

という引き金文を口にした後

「彼は」というキューが与えられます。

練習する人は引き金文を

He goes to the library every day.

と変化させます。次に、

「昨日」というキューが与えられると、今度は

He went to the library yesterday.

という文を作ります。

　パターン・プラクティスでは、このようにして、先行の文を少しずつ変化させながら、次々と新しい文を作っていきます。「どんどん話すための瞬間英作文トレーニング」「スラスラ話すための瞬間英作文シャッフルトレーニング」では、独立した日本語文を英語に変えていく手法を採用しています。これもパターン・プラクティスのバリエーションと言えますが、本書では、大部分をパターン・プラクティスのより基本的な方法である、前の文を少しずつ変えていく手法で瞬間英作文トレーニングを行います。

　流行り廃りは世の常で、外国語学習法の世界も例外ではありません。数十年前、隆盛を見たパターン・プラクティスですが、現在では、時代遅れの学習法とみなされる傾向があり、これを取り扱った教材は非常に少なくなってしまいました。しかし、流行とトレーニングの効果には直接の関係はありません。パターン・プラクティスが廃れてしまったのは、それ自体に効果がなかったのではなく、その効果を享受できる前にトレーニングを止めてしまう人が多かったというだけのことです。

どんな学習法でも、効果が得られるまでには、多少の努力・我慢が必要です。しかし、しっかりとした学習法であれば、一定期間継続すれば、必ず相応の効果が得られるものです。パターン・プラクティスもそうした確かな学習法の一つです。流行した時代から現在に至るまで、継続実行した人は大きな効果と、次の段階の学習に移っていく確かな足掛かりを得ていったのです。

　かくいう私も、パターン・プラクティスから大きな恩恵を受けた一人です。瞬間英作文トレーニングを開始した当初、パターン・プラクティストレーニングを盛んに行いました。私がトレーニングを行った1980年代でも、パターン・プラクティスは、学習法としては既に骨董品扱いでした。ただ、簡単な英文が反射的に口から出ないことを自覚し、自分の中に瞬間英作文回路を作ることを当面の目標にした私には、非常に有用なメソッドに思えました。そして、予想通り、パターン・プラクティストレーニングは短期間で私の文型操作能力を大きく伸ばしてくれました。基礎がしっかりしたことで、私自身の瞬間英作文トレーニングは、日本語の短文をそっくり英文に換えるものに移行しました。前の文を微妙に変えていく基本的パターン・プラクティスでは、負荷がほとんどなくなったことと、私自身の好みもありました。その後もこの日本文をそっくり英文に変えるトレーニングを中心にして、瞬間英作文回路を完成させました。

自分の英語塾を立ち上げ指導するようになってからも、瞬間英作文トレーニングとしては、主に「日本文→英文」の短文英作の教材を使用、あるいは作成してきました。概ね効果は上々でしたが、生徒の数が増していくにつれ、一部に、このトレーニングで効果が上がりにくい人も出てきました。次のような点が主要な原因でした。

① 自発的な発言でない引き金の日本文を読み解くのに戸惑ったり、抵抗を感じる。
② 日本文の内容のイメージ化がスムーズにいかない。
③ 文型の操作感が掴めず、単に英文を表面的に暗記してしまう。

要約すれば、「日本語に振り回されてしまう」ということです。

ある外国語を習得するのに、その言語だけで学習を行うのは理想です。しかし、初期段階からこれを行うのは至難です。例えば、英語を話す力をつけるのに、独り言を英語で言い続けるという方法があります。目に映ること、頭に浮かぶことを片端から英語にしていくということですが、これは上級者用のトレーニングです。初級段階でこれを行おうとすると、文型、語彙のストックが少なすぎて、始めた途端、失語状態に陥ってしまいます。話す力の基礎となる文型操作力をつけるには、それらの文型を使って膨大な数の文を作ることが必須です。これを実行するためには学習初期には、やはり、母語＝日本語を引き金にするのが得策です。

　しかし、補助輪として使うはずの日本語そのものに引きずり回されてしまうとなると本末転倒です。こうした生徒達に対して、私はパターン・プラクティスをやってもらうことにしました。パターン・プラクティスなら、元の文を少しずつ変えていくだけなので、日本語の影響は最小限に抑えることができるからです。

　しかし、いかんせん現在パターン・プラクティスのテキストが少ない上に、基本レベルの文型に絞り、かつ、まんべんなくカバーしたものとなると極端に数が限られてしまいます。市販の教材でトレーニングしてもらいながら、大急ぎで、現場の必要に合うオリジナル教材を作成していきました。反応は非常に良く、日本文→英文の瞬間英作文トレーニングに抵抗を示したり、努力していても結果がはかばかしくなかった生徒達が大きな進歩をし始めました。彼らのトレーニングの消化スピードも急上昇し、私は教材を書き足していくのに大わらわという状態になってしまいました。

特に数人の生徒の大躍進は印象的でした。彼らは皆非常に努力をするタイプで、瞬間英作文トレーニングをするとテキストに出てくる英文は、じきにスラスラと言えるようになるのですが、瞬間英作文回路そのもののチェックをするために、元の文をすこしでも変化させると、途端に口が重くなったり、極めて初歩的なミスを繰り返してしまうのです。つまり、答えの英文を丸暗記してしまっていたのです。これについては、御本人たちも自覚症状があったようです。しかし、問題点の特定とその解決はイコールではありません。突破口を見つけるために、教師も生徒もしばし頭を抱えることとなってしまいました。ところが、パターン・プラクティスの手法を使うことによって、急速に症状が改善されていったのです。彼らの進歩の速度は私がパターン・プラクティス教材を書き足していくペースを上回ってしまい、まもなく与える教材がなくなってしまったのですが、その時には日本語→英語タイプの瞬間英作文トレーニングでも、単なる暗記をしてしまう癖がなくなり、十分に効果を上げることができるようになったのです。同時に、伸び悩んでいたリスニング力やTOEICのスコアも上昇していきました。これは驚くことではありませんでした。英語力の各側面は有機的に繋がっていますから、基本文型が感覚的に身につけば、英語力全体が底上げされるのです。

　せっかく苦労して作成した教材ということで、日本文→英文の瞬間英作文トレーニングに問題のない生徒にも、異なった刺激を与える意味で、パターン・プラクティスを時折やってもらいました。すると思いがけないほど、このトレーニングは人気を博しました。その手軽さ、負荷の軽さから単位時間内に作れる英文数が増え、そこ

から得られるスピード感がその理由だったのでしょう。

　また、私の生徒のほとんどはパターン・プラクティスという学習法やその手法を初めて知ったということでした。外国語学習法の趨勢の中で、久しく光を当てられず、埃を被っていた感のあるパターン・プラクティスは、「古くて新しい」効果的なメソッドと言えるでしょう。

本書の構成とステージ進行における位置づけ

　本書は、基礎編と発展編の2部構成になっています。前半の基礎編では、中学2年前半レベルくらいまでの文型の練習をします。文型ごとの構成ではありませんが、be動詞だけの文、一般動詞だけの文と、単純なものから始まり、be動詞、一般動詞の交互に現れる練習、疑問詞の導入と、先に進むにつれ、雪だるま式に新たな要素が加わっていきます。基礎編では、現在完了導入の項を除き、表題はついていません。使用文型は基礎的なもので負荷も軽いので、スピード感を得るため、1項目あたりの文数15文とやや多めです。

　応用編では、中学2年中盤以降から3年にかけて学習するレベルの文型を、個々に練習していきます。各項に練習対象となる文型が示されています。文型の難度が上がりますので、1項目あたりの文数は12に下がります。

　私は、学習効率の点から、瞬間英作文トレーニングを3つのステージに分けて行うことをお勧めしています。各ステージの達成目標、トレーニング内容は次のようなものです。

第 1 ステージ
目的：瞬間英作文の基礎回路の養成。
トレーニング内容：
> 文型別に編纂された例文集で、口頭で英作文練習をおこなう。使用されている語彙に知らないものがない簡単な文でできているテキストを用いることが重要。

第 2 ステージ
目的：瞬間英作文回路の完成。
トレーニング内容：
> 文型へのアクセス能力をつけるために練習問題が文型別に並んでいない、文型シャッフルされた素材を使用する。

第 3 ステージ
目的：表現力の拡大
トレーニング内容：
> 第 2 ステージまでで完成した瞬間英作文回路を使用して、多くの文を楽にスピーディーに作る中で、使用語彙・フレーズを増やす。

　本書の基本編は、文型ごとに項目を立てていないので、第 2 ステージの性質が強く、発展編では、文型ごとに項目を立てていますので、第 1 ステージのトレーニングと言えます。しかし、基本編、発展編ともに、先行する文を元にして微妙に変えていくパターン・プラクティスの性質上、負荷は少なく、スピード感のあるトレーニングとなるでしょう。つまり、本書は、第 1 ステージと第 2 ステージを横断的に、より軽い負荷で、スピードに乗ってトレーニングする

テキストと言えるでしょう。また、文型・文法の学習書ではなく、扱う文型が既に理解できていることを前提に、それらの文型を実際に使うトレーニングブックであるという点は、「どんどん話すための瞬間英作トレーニング」「スラスラ話すための瞬間英作文シャッフルトレーニング」と同様です。

本書の使い方

　本書では、前の文を指示に従い少しずつ変えながら、連続的に英文を作っていく練習をしていきます。

　実際の練習問題を例に使い、練習してみましょう。

　基本編の7では、まず

①彼は毎月アメリカに行く。

という引き金文が与えられますので、それに対し、

He goes to America every month.

という英文を口頭で作ります。次に、

②　　　先月

というキューが与えられると、「先月」というフレーズによって時制が過去になるので

He went to America last month.

を作ります。次に、

③　　　　　　　　　行きましたか？

と疑問文を誘導するキューにより、

Did he go to America last month?

という疑問文を作ります。次に、

④彼らは　　　　　　　来月

というキューにより、主語と時制が変化して、

Will they go to America next month?

という英文になります。

　このように、先行する文をできるだけ維持しながら、与えられるキューが要求する変化を加え新たな文を連続的に作っていくのが、本書のトレーニングの基本です。

　今例に挙げた基本編の7のように、完全な文として「引き金文が」与えられるのは、冒頭の1文だけという形式の他、1項目中で、複数の「引き金文」が現れる項目もあります。

例えば、発展編の「従属節―1」では、

① 私が朝起きた時、晴れていた。

で最初の引き金文が与えられ、
②、③ではフレーズによるキューでこの引き金文からの派生文を作りますが、次に、

④彼が帰ったとき、奥さんは夕食を料理していました。

と新たな引き金文が与えられます。
　このようにして、この項目では、合計4つの引き金文が現れます。引き金文が新たに出る場合には、比較的大きな変化をつけることと、「どんどん話すための瞬間英作文トレーニング」「スラスラ話すための瞬間英作文シャッフルトレーニング」で行った、丸ごと日本語文→英文の英作練習をしてアクセントをつけることができます。

　引き金文やキューに従って英文を作る時、最初は間違えたり、とつとつとした口調になることが多いでしょう。その際、自然な口調で言えるまで、何度か英文を繰り返してください。決して丸暗記をしようとはせず、英文の意味を理解しながら、その場、口に落ちつければいいだけです。テキストの最後まで終わったら、また冒頭に戻り同じように練習していきます。これを、「サイクルを回す」と言います。サイクル回しが進むにつれ、英文を指示に従い変化させる

ことが楽になっていくでしょう。

＊引き金文とそれを変化させるためのキューは基本的に日本語ですが、発展編 1～4 の受動態と 26～27 の文から関係代名詞節への変換では、英文を引き金文として用いています。

＊付属 CD の使い方

　本書には練習用のポーズ付き CD がついています。最初は、テキストを見ながら、発音・イントネーションを確かめるために使い、サイクル回しが進み、慣れてきたら CD 音声のみを使った練習をしてみると、テキストを見ながらのトレーニングとは異なる刺激の練習、より実践的な練習をすることができるでしょう。

本書でトレーニングする上での注意点

　パターン・プラクティスは、短い語句をキューとして使うことにより日本語の使用を最小限にとどめ、機械的な暗記を防いだり、負荷を軽くする利点があります。しかし、一方で、キューが短いため、練習問題の意図と違う英文を作ってしまうことが起こりやすくなります。

　例えば、

He talked to her.　（彼は彼女と話しました。）

という文の後のキューが「話しませんでした」の時、否定文にする以外、元の文を維持するので、答えの文は、

He didn't talk to her.

となるのですが、思わず、He didn't talk. としてしまったりします。同じように、

He is kind to old people.（彼はお年寄りに親切です。）

に対するキュー「親切ですか？」に反応して、Is he kind?という英文を作り、前の文の、to old people を落としてしまったりするかもしれません。

トレーニングの序盤では、こういう躓きが多く起こり、スピード感を得られず、ちょっといらいらすることがあるかもしれません。しかし、多少テキストの答えと違う英文を作ってしまっても、それが正しい英文であるなら、瞬間英作文回路を作る上で、プラスにこそなれマイナスになることはありません。あまり、気にせず本線に戻るように答えの英文を口に落ちつけ、トレーニングを続けてください。サイクルを回し、テキストに慣れるにつれて、こうした躓き、戸惑いは、どんどん少なくなっていきます。こうなれば、流れに乗り、パターン・プラクティスならではの軽い負荷のトレーニンが順調に進んでいくでしょう。

瞬間英作文 パターン・プラクティスのやり方

「引き金」の日本文でまず文単位の英作文

短い日本語のキューで元の文を次々に変えていきます

再び「引き金文」が現われ文が大きく変わります

15 快速トレーニング ⑮

DISC1 TRACK 15

1 彼は自転車で学校に行きます。
2 　　　　　　　　　　　行きますか？
3 　　　　どのように
4 あなたは　　　　　会社 (the office) に
5 　　　車で　　　　　　行くのですか？
6 　　　なぜ
7 あなたの御主人は
8 私はその時幸せでした。
9 　　　　　　　　　　自分の部屋にいました。
10 あなたは　　　　　　　　いましたか？
11 　　　　　　　　　彼女に電話しましたか？
12 　　　いつ
13 彼は
14 　　　　　　　　　その本を買いましたか。
15 　　　　　　　　　買うのでしょうか？ (未来)

58

文字によるトレーニングと併行してCDで音声に反応するトレーニングを行います

26

CD

日本語（一部英語）のキュー⇨ポーズ⇨英文

ここで瞬間英作文！

1. He goes to school by bicycle.
2. Does he go to school by bicycle?
3. How does he go to school?
4. How do you go to the office?
5. Do you go to the office by car?
6. Why do you go to the office by car?
7. Why does your hasband go to the office by car?
8. I was happy then.
9. I was in my room then.
10. Were you in your room then?
11. Did you call her then?
12. When did you call her?
13. When did he call her?
14. When did he buy the book?
15. When will he buy the book?

英文を作ったら、口に落ち着くまで何度か軽く繰り返します

おはよう！　レトロだねぇ

＊本書はすでに知っている文型を、実際に使えるようにするトレーニング・ブックです。中学レベルの文型の学習は終わっていることを前提にしています。

基礎編

1 快速トレーニング ①

DISC 1 TRACK 01

① 私は大学生です。

② 彼女は　　　　　　　　　　　ですか？

③ あなたは　　　高校生

④ 彼らは　　　　　　　　　　　ではないのですか？

⑤ あの少女たちは　　　　　　　ですか？

⑥ 　　　　　　　可愛いです。

⑦ あの猫は

⑧ 　　　　　　　私の (もの) です。

⑨ 　　　　　　　あなたの (もの) ですか？

⑩ この辞書は

⑪ 　　　　　　　厚いです。

⑫ 　　　　　　　安く (cheap) ありません。

⑬ この本は

⑭ 　　　　　　　役に立ち (useful) ます。

⑮ この機械は

ぜんぜん可愛くない

1. I am a college student.
2. Is she a college student?
3. Are you a high school student?
4. Aren't they high school students?
5. Are those girls high school students?
6. Those girls are pretty.
7. That cat is pretty.
8. That cat is mine.
9. Is that cat yours?
10. Is this dictionary yours?
11. This dictionary is thick.
12. This dictionary isn't cheap.
13. This book isn't cheap.
14. This book is useful.
15. This machine is useful.

2 快速トレーニング ②

DISC 1　TRACK 02

① トムはその本を読みました。

②　　　　　　　　　　　　読みましたか？

③ あなたは

④　　　　　その小説 (novel) を

⑤ 彼は

⑥　　　　　　　　　　　　読むでしょうか？（未来）

⑦　　　　　　　　　　　　読むでしょう。

⑧　　　　　あの家に住んでいます。

⑨　　　　　　　　　　　　住んでいますか？

⑩ ブラウン一家 (the Browns) は

⑪ 彼女の兄は

⑫　　　　日本に

⑬　　　　彼らを知っています。

⑭　　　　　　　　　　　知っていますか？

⑮ 彼女のご両親は

1. Tom read the book.
2. Did Tom read the book?
3. Did you read the book?
4. Did you read the novel?
5. Did he read the novel?
6. Will he read the novel?
7. He will read the novel.
8. He lives in that house.
9. Does he live in that house?
10. Do the Browns live in that house?
11. Does her brother live in that house?
12. Does her brother live in Japan?
13. Her brother knows them.
14. Does her brother know them?
15. Do her parents know them?

3 快速トレーニング ③

DISC 1　TRACK 03

① 私は英語を勉強します。

② 彼は

③ 　　　　　　　　　　　しますか？

④ 　　　　日本語を

⑤ 　　　　彼女を知っています。

⑥ 　　　　彼女に親切です。

⑦ 　　　　彼女に親切ですか？

⑧ 　　　　彼女が好きですか？

⑨ あなたは

⑩ ボブは

⑪ 　　　　　　　　　好きでした。

⑫ 　　　　　　　　　好きになるでしょう。（未来）

⑬ みんなが

⑭ 　　　　明日　　　ここに来るでしょう。

⑮ 　　　　　　　　　ここにいるでしょう。

1. I study English.
2. He studies English.
3. Does he study English?
4. Does he study Japanese?
5. He knows her.
6. He is kind to her.
7. Is he kind to her?
8. Does he like her?
9. Do you like her?
10. Does Bob like her?
11. Bob liked her.
12. Bob will like her.
13. Everyone will like her.
14. Everyone will come here tomorrow.
15. Everyone will be here tomorrow.

4 快速トレーニング ④

DISC 1　TRACK 04

1. 彼の家は大きい。
2. 　　　　　　大きいですか？
3. 　　　　　　大きくありません。
4. 彼の奥さんは
5. 　　　　　　美しいです。
6. 　　　　　　英語を話します。
7. 彼女の子供たちは
8. 　　　　　　話しますか？
9. 　　　　　　大学生ですか？
10. あなたのお兄さんは
11. 　　　　　　弁護士ですか？
12. 　　　　　　弁護士になるでしょう。（未来）
13. ナンシーのご主人は
14. 　　　　　　数学を教えていました。
15. 　　　　　　教えていましたか？

1. His house is big.

2. Is his house big?

3. His house isn't big.

4. His wife isn't big.

5. His wife is beautiful.

6. His wife speaks English.

7. Her children speak English.

8. Do her children speak English?

9. Are her children college students?

10. Is your brother a college student?

11. Is your brother a lawyer?

12. Your brother will be a lawyer.

13. Nancy's husband will be a lawyer.

14. Nancy's husband taught mathematics.

15. Did Nancy's husband teach mathematics?

5 快速トレーニング ⑤

DISC 1　TRACK 05

① あなたは映画が好きですか？

② あなたのお母さんは

③ 　　　　　　看護師ですか？

④ 彼の奥さんは

⑤ 　　　　　　中国語を話しますか？

⑥ 　　　　　　背が高いです。

⑦ 彼の子供たちは

⑧ 　　　　　　昨日ここに来ましたか？

⑨ 　　　　　　明日

⑩ 　　　　　　　　　　　　家にいるでしょうか？

⑪ 　　　　　　　　　　　　　　いないでしょう。

⑫ トムとボブは

⑬ 　　　　　　昨晩

⑭ 　　　　　　　　　　　　映画に行きましたか？

⑮ 　　　　　　いつも　　　　幸せです。

1. Do you like movies?

2. Does your mother like movies?

3. Is your mother a nurse?

4. Is his wife a nurse?

5. Does his wife speak Chinese?

6. His wife is tall.

7. His children are tall.

8. Did his children come here yesterday?

9. Will his children come here tomorrow?

10. Will his children be at home tomorrow?

11. His children won't be at home tomorrow.

12. Tom and Bob won't be at home tomorrow.

13. Tom and Bob weren't at home last night.

14. Did Tom and Bob go to the movies last night?

15. Tom and Bob are always happy.

快速トレーニング ⑥

DISC 1　TRACK 06

① 彼は英語を話す。

②　　　　　　　　　　　　　　話しますか？

③ 彼女たちは

④　　　　　日本語を　　　　　話します。

⑤ トムは　　　　　　上手に

⑥　　　　　　　　　　　　　　話しません。

⑦　　　　　内気 (shy) です。

⑧ エミリーは

⑨　　　　　昨日　　　　　　　図書館に行きました。

⑩　　　　　明日

⑪ あなたは　　　　　　　　　　行くのですか？

⑫　　　　　　　　　　　　　　家にいますか？

⑬ 彼は

⑭　　　　　1時間前　　　　　　いませんでした。

⑮　　　　　　　　　　　　　　ここに来ました。

1. He speaks English.

2. Does he speak English?

3. Do they speak English?

4. They speak Japanese.

5. Tom speaks Japanese well.

6. Tom doesn't speak Japanese well.

7. Tom is shy.

8. Emily is shy.

9. Emily went to the library yesterday.

10. Emily will go to the library tomorrow.

11. Will you go to the library tomorrow?

12. Will you be at home tomorrow?

13. Will he be at home tomorrow?

14. He wasn't at home an hour ago.

15. He came here an hour ago.

7 快速トレーニング ⑦

DISC 1 TRACK 07

1. 彼は毎月アメリカに行く。
2. 　　　　　　先月
3. 　　　　　　　　　　　　　行きましたか？
4. 彼らは　　　来月
5. 彼らの息子さんは
6. 彼は　　　　　　　　　　　行きます。
7. トムは　　　来年
8. 　　　　　　　　　　　　　12歳になります。
9. 　　　　　　今　　　　　　11歳です。
10. 　　　　　　去年　　　　　10歳でした。
11. 　　　　　　毎日　　　　　ピアノを弾きます。
12. 　　　　　　昨日
13. 　　　　　　　　　　　　　病気でしたか？
14. 　　　　　　　　　　　　　ピアノを弾きましたか？
15. あなたは　　　　　　　　　バイオリンを

1. He goes to America every month.

2. He went to America last month.

3. Did he go to America last month?

4. Will they go to America next month?

5. Will their son go to America next month?

6. He will go to America next month.

7. Tom will go to America next year.

8. Tom will be twelve years old next year.

9. Tom is eleven years old now.

10. Tom was ten years old last year.

11. Tom plays the piano every day.

12. Tom played the piano yesterday.

13. Was Tom sick yesterday?

14. Did Tom play the piano yesterday?

15. Did you play the violin yesterday?

8 快速トレーニング ⑧

DISC 1　TRACK 08

① 私は彼にその本をあげた。

② 　　　　　　　　　　　　　　あげよう。（未来）

③ あなたは　　　　　　　　　　あげるのですか？

④ 　　　　　　　　　　　　　　あげましたか？

⑤ 　　　彼女に　　花を

⑥ 彼は　　　　　　　　　　　　あげました。

⑦ 　　　　　　　その写真を　　見せました。

⑧ 私は　　彼らに

⑨ 　　　　　　　日本語を　　　教えました。

⑩ 　　　　　　　フランス語を　教えるでしょう。（未来）

⑪ あなたは　　　　　　　　　　教えますか？

⑫ 　　　　　　　スペイン語を　教えたのですか？

⑬ 私は　　　　　　　　　　　　教えた。

⑭ 　　　　　　　その話をした（語った）。

⑮ 　　　彼女に　　その知らせ（the news）を

1. I gave him the book.
2. I will give him the book.
3. Will you give him the book?
4. Did you give him the book?
5. Did you give her flowers?
6. He gave her flowers.
7. He showed her the picture.
8. I showed them the picture.
9. I taught them Japanese.
10. I will teach them French.
11. Will you teach them French?
12. Did you teach them Spanish?
13. I taught them Spanish.
14. I told them the story.
15. I told her the news.

快速トレーニング ⑨

DISC 1 · TRACK 09

① 彼女は幸せだった。

② 幸せでしたか？

③ 日本語を話しましたか？

④ 怒っていますか？

⑤ 怒っていません。

⑥ 怒るでしょう。

⑦ 内気です。

⑧ 彼らは

⑨ ロバートは

⑩ 数学を勉強しました。

⑪ 教えます。

⑫ 子供たちに

⑬ 親切です。

⑭ 女性に

⑮ 彼らは　老人に (old people)

1. She was happy.

2. Was she happy?

3. Did she speak Japanese?

4. Is she angry?

5. She isn't angry.

6. She will be angry.

7. She is shy.

8. They are shy.

9. Robert is shy.

10. Robert studied mathematics.

11. Robert teaches mathematics.

12. Robert teaches mathematics to children.

13. Robert is kind to children.

14. Robert is kind to women.

15. They are kind to old people.

おみ足が汚れます!

10 快速トレーニング ⑩

DISC 1 TRACK 10

① 彼女は毎日夕食を料理する。

② トムは　　　　　　　　料理しますか？

③ 　　　昨日　　　　　　しましたか？

④ 彼らは　明日

⑤ 　　　　　　　　　　　野球をするでしょう。

⑥ 　　　　　　　　　　　学校に行くでしょうか？

⑦ 彼女は　　　　　　　　パーティーに

⑧ 　　　昨夜　　　　　　　　　　行きました。

⑨ ボブは　　　　　　　　　　　　　行きませんでした。

⑩ 　　　一昨日　　　　　図書館に行った。

⑪ 　　　毎朝　　　　　　シャワーを浴びる。

⑫ 　　　その時　　　　　　　　浴びていました。

⑬ 私の弟は　今

⑭ 　　　毎日　　　　　　散歩をします。

⑮ 　　　当時は毎日（当時 in those days）

1. She cooks dinner every day.
2. Does Tom cook dinner every day?
3. Did Tom cook dinner yesterday?
4. Will they cook dinner tomorrow?
5. They will play baseball tomorrow.
6. Will they go to school tomorrow?
7. Will she go to the party tomorrow?
8. She went to the party last night.
9. Bob didn't go to the party last night.
10. Bob went to the library the day before yesterday.
11. Bob takes a shower every morning.
12. Bob was taking a shower then.
13. My brother is taking a shower now.
14. My brother takes a walk every day.
15. My brother took a walk every day in those days.

快速トレーニング ⑪

DISC 1 TRACK 11

① あなたは何を買ったのですか？

② 　　　　　　　読んでいるのですか？

③ エミリーは

④ 　　　　　　なぜ幸福なのですか？

⑤ 　　　　　　なぜ彼を愛しているのですか？

⑥ 　　　　　　なぜ彼とそこへ行ったのですか？

⑦ 彼らはどこにいますか？

⑧ 　　　　どこに行ったのですか？

⑨ 　　　　どこに住んでいますか？

⑩ 　　　　明日どこに泊まるのでしょうか？

⑪ トムはいつ勉強しますか？

⑫ 　　　　いつ帰ってくるでしょうか？

⑬ 　　　　いつ結婚しましたか？

⑭ 　　　　いつ日本を発ちましたか？

⑮ 　　　　いつ日本に帰ってきましたか？

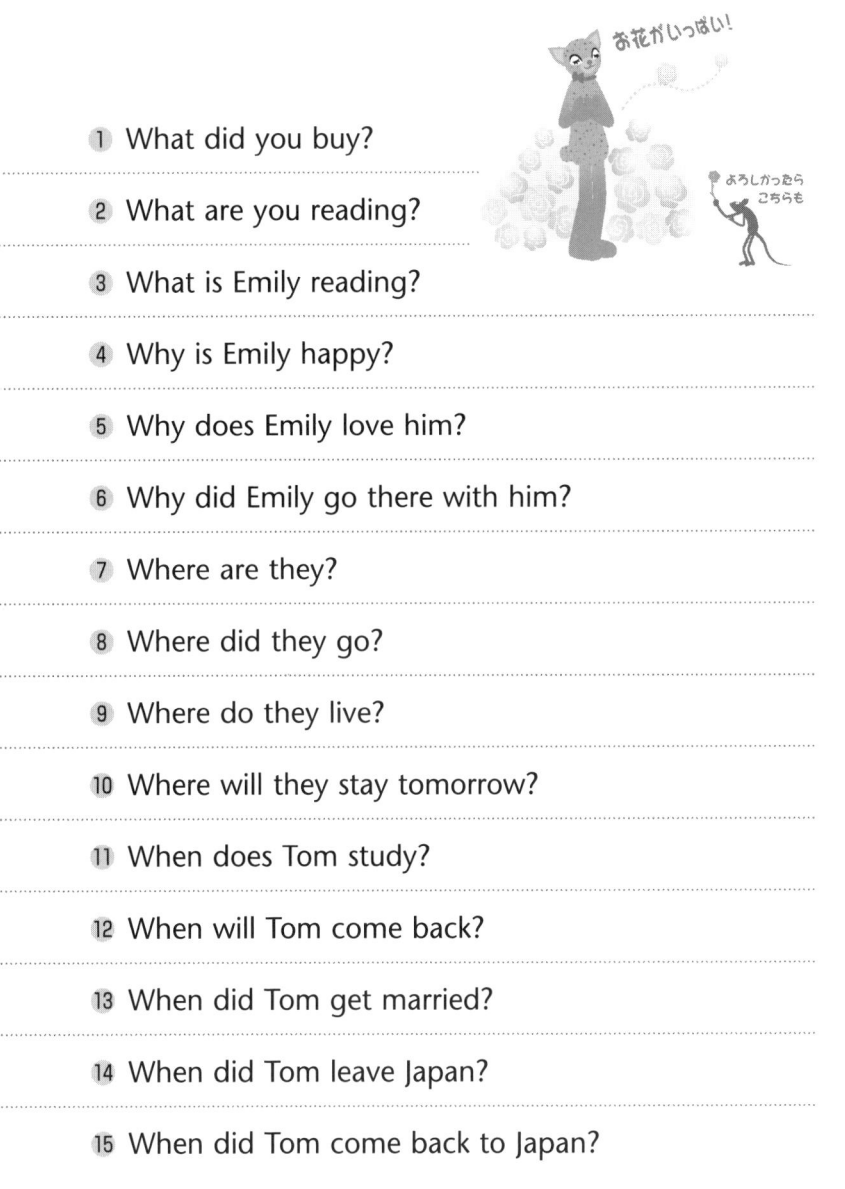

1. What did you buy?
2. What are you reading?
3. What is Emily reading?
4. Why is Emily happy?
5. Why does Emily love him?
6. Why did Emily go there with him?
7. Where are they?
8. Where did they go?
9. Where do they live?
10. Where will they stay tomorrow?
11. When does Tom study?
12. When will Tom come back?
13. When did Tom get married?
14. When did Tom leave Japan?
15. When did Tom come back to Japan?

12 快速トレーニング ⑫

DISC 1　TRACK 12

1. どちらがあなたの車ですか？

2. 　　　　彼らの家ですか？

3. どちらの本があなたは欲しいですか？

4. どちらの花を

5. 　　　　　　　彼女は買うでしょうか？

6. 誰がこの部屋を使いますか？

7. 　　窓を割ったのですか？

8. 　　彼女と一緒にいたのですか？

9. これは誰の自転車ですか？

10. 　　誰の鉛筆ですか？

11. あれらは

12. この辞書はだれのものですか？

13. これらのノートは

14. あなたはどうやってフランス語を覚えましたか？

15. 　　　　　　　この問題を解き (solve) ましたか？

1. Which is your car?
2. Which is their house?
3. Which book do you want?
4. Which flower do you want?
5. Which flower will she buy?
6. Who uses this room?
7. Who broke the window?
8. Who was with her?
9. Whose bicycle is this?
10. Whose pencil is this?
11. Whose pencils are those?
12. Whose is this dictionary?
13. Whose are these notebooks?
14. How did you learn French?
15. How did you solve this problem?

13 快速トレーニング ⑬

DISC 1　TRACK 13

① 彼は朝食にパンを食べました。

② 　　　　　　　　　　何を食べましたか？

③ 僕は　　　　　　　　パンを食べた。

④ 彼は彼女に会った。

⑤ 　　　　　　　　　　会いましたか？

⑥ どこで　　　　　　　会いましたか？

⑦ 　　　　　　　　　　勉強しますか？

⑧ 　　　　　　　　　　どこにいますか？

⑨ 　　明日

⑩ 　　　　　　　　　　うちにいますか？

⑪ 彼は　昨日

⑫ 　　　　　　エミリーと　　公園に行きました。

⑬ トムは　毎日曜　　　　　　　　行きます。

⑭ 　　来週　　　　　　映画に行きます。

⑮ 　　昨夜　　　　（エミリーと）一緒にいましたか？

① He ate bread for breakfast.

② What did he eat for breakfast?

③ I ate bread for breakfast.

④ He met her.

⑤ Did he meet her?

⑥ Where did he meet her?

⑦ Where does he study?

⑧ Where is he?

⑨ Where will he be tomorrow?

⑩ Will he be at home tomorrow?

⑪ Was he at home yesterday?

⑫ He went to the park with Emily yesterday.

⑬ Tom goes to the park with Emily every Sunday.

⑭ Tom will go to the movies with Emily next week.

⑮ Was Tom with Emily last night?

14 快速トレーニング ⑭

DISC 1　TRACK 14

1. 僕は彼女にりんごをあげました。

2. あなたは　　　　　　　　　あげましたか？

3. 　　　何を

4. 彼は　　　　　　　　　　あげるでしょうか？（未来）

5. 　　　　弟に　　　　　　あげましたか？

6. 　　　　（弟に）親切ですか？

7. トムは宿題をしましたか？

8. 私は　　　　　　　　　　しませんでした。

9. なぜあなたは　　　　　　しなかったのですか？

10. 　　　　　　　　　　　　泣いたのですか？

11. 　　　　　　　　　　　　怒っていたのですか？

12. 　　　彼は　　　　　　怒っているのですか？

13. 　　　　　　　　　　　　英語を勉強するのですか？

14. 　　　彼女は

15. どうやって　　　　　　覚えたのですか？

1. I gave her an apple.

2. Did you give her an apple?

3. What did you give her?

4. What will he give her?

5. What did he give his brother?

6. Is he kind to his brother?

7. Did Tom do his homework?

8. I didn't do my homework.

9. Why didn't you do your homework?

10. Why did you cry?

11. Why were you angry?

12. Why is he angry?

13. Why does he study English?

14. Why does she study English?

15. How did she learn English?

15 快速トレーニング ⑮

DISC 1 TRACK 15

① 彼は自転車で学校に行きます。

② 　　　　　　　　　　　行きますか？

③ 　　　　　どのように

④ あなたは　　　　　　　　会社 (the office) に

⑤ 　　　　　車で　　　　　　　　　行くのですか？

⑥ 　　　なぜ

⑦ あなたの御主人は

⑧ 私はその時幸せでした。

⑨ 　　　　　　　　　　自分の部屋にいました。

⑩ あなたは　　　　　　　　　　　いましたか？

⑪ 　　　　　　　　　　彼女に電話しましたか？

⑫ 　　　　いつ

⑬ 彼は

⑭ 　　　　　　　　　　その本を買いましたか？

⑮ 　　　　　　　　　　買うのでしょうか？（未来）

1. He goes to school by bicycle.

2. Does he go to school by bicycle?

3. How does he go to school?

4. How do you go to the office?

5. Do you go to the office by car?

6. Why do you go to the office by car?

7. Why does your husband go to the office by car?

8. I was happy then.

9. I was in my room then.

10. Were you in your room then?

11. Did you call her then?

12. When did you call her?

13. When did he call her?

14. When did he buy the book?

15. When will he buy the book?

16 快速トレーニング ⑯

DISC 1　TRACK 16

① エミリーは自分の部屋にいます。

②　　　　　　１時間前

③　　　　　　明日　　　　　　ニューヨークに

④ あなたは　　　　　　　　　　　　　　いるのですか？

⑤ 彼らは　　昨日

⑥　　　　　　　　　　　日本を発ちましたか？

⑦ 彼の両親は　　　　　　　　発ちました。

⑧　　　　　　いつ

⑨ 彼女は　　　　　　　　彼と結婚し (marry) ましたか？

⑩　　　　　　なぜ

⑪　　　　　　　　　　　泣いているのですか？

⑫ 彼らは

⑬ エミリーは今朝シャワーを浴びました。

⑭　　　　　　毎朝　　　　　　　　浴びます。

⑮　　　　　　毎晩　　　　トムに電話します。

いつ結婚したの？
覚えとらん

1. Emily is in her room.

2. Emily was in her room an hour ago.

3. Emily will be in New York tomorrow.

4. Will you be in New York tomorrow?

5. Were they in New York yesterday?

6. Did they leave Japan yesterday?

7. His parents left Japan yesterday.

8. When did his parents leave Japan?

9. When did she marry him?

10. Why did she marry him?

11. Why is she crying?

12. Why are they crying?

13. Emily took a shower this morning.

14. Emily takes a shower every morning.

15. Emily calls Tom every night.

17 現在完了—1 完了

DISC 1　TRACK 17

1. 私はまだ朝食を食べていません。

2. あなたは　　　　　　　　　　　もう食べましたか？

3. 彼女は　　　　夕食を

4. 　　　　　　もう宿題をしましたか？

5. トムは　　　　　　　　　　　まだしていません。

6. 彼らは

7. 　　　　　もう出発しましたか？

8. トムとボブは

9. 　　　　　まだ出発していません。

10. 　　　　　窓を割ってしまいました。

11. 　　　　　　割ってしまったのですか？

12. 誰が

13. 僕は　　　　割ってしまいました。

14. 　　　　もうすべての本を読んでしまいました。

15. あなたは　　もう読んでしまったのですか？

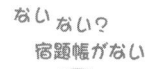

1. I haven't had (eaten) breakfast yet.

2. Have you had (eaten) breakfast yet?

3. Has she had (eaten) dinner yet?

4. Has she done her homework yet?

5. Tom hasn't done his homework yet.

6. They haven't done their homework yet.

7. Have they left yet?

8. Have Tom and Bob left yet?

9. Tom and Bob haven't left yet.

10. Tom and Bob have broken the window.

11. Have Tom and Bob broken the window?

12. Who has broken the window?

13. I have broken the window.

14. I have already read all the books.

15. Have you already read all the books?

18 現在完了—2 継続

DISC 1 TRACK 18

1. 私はこの町に 10 年住んでいます。

2. あなたは　　　　　　　　　　住んでいるのですか？

3. 彼は　ニューヨークに

4. 　　　どのくらい（長く）

5. 彼らは　　　　　　　　日本に

6. 　　　長くは　　　　　住んでいません。

7. 　　　　　　　　　　　彼女を待ってはいません。

8. 　　　5 年　　　　　　結婚しています。

9. トムとエミリーは

10. 　　　どのくらい（長く）　結婚しているのですか？

11. 　　　　　　　　　　　友人ですか？

12. 　　　2 時間　　　　　テレビを見ています。

13. 彼女の弟は

14. 　　　　　　　　　　　ここにいるのですか？

15. 　　　どのくらい

1. I have lived in this town for ten years.

2. Have you lived in this town for ten years?

3. Has he lived in New York for ten years?

4. How long has he lived in New York?

5. How long have they lived in Japan?

6. They haven't lived in Japan for a long time.

7. They haven't been waiting for her for a long time.

8. They have been married for five years.

9. Tom and Emily have been married for five years.

10. How long have Tom and Emily been married?

11. How long have Tom and Emily been friends?

12. Tom and Emily have been watching TV for two hours.

13. Her brother has been watching TV for two hours.

14. Has her brother been here for two hours?

15. How long has her brother been here?

19 現在完了—3 経験

DISC 1) TRACK 19

① わたしは一度彼に会ったことがあります。

② 彼女は

③　　　　今までに　　　　　　　　　　ありますか？

④　　　　　　　　ピアノを弾いたことが

⑤　　　　　　　　アメリカに行ったことが

⑥ 彼らは

⑦　　　　以前に　　　　　　行ったことがあります。

⑧　　　　　　　　ヨーロッパに

⑨ エミリーとナンシーは　何度も (many times)

⑩　　　　今までに　この映画を見たことがありますか？

⑪　　　　　　一度も　　　　見たことがありません。

⑫ トムは

⑬　　　　　　　　この車を運転したことが

⑭　　　　今までに　　　　　　　　　　ありますか？

⑮　　　　　　　　彼女と話したことが

1. I have met him once.

2. She has met him once.

3. Has she ever met him?

4. Has she ever played the piano?

5. Has she ever been to America?

6. Have they ever been to America?

7. They have been to America before.

8. They have been to Europe before.

9. Emily and Nancy have been to Europe many times.

10. Have Emily and Nancy ever seen this movie?

11. Emily and Nancy have never seen this movie.

12. Tom has never seen this movie.

13. Tom has never driven this car.

14. Has Tom ever driven this car?

15. Has Tom ever talked to her?

20 快速トレーニング ⑰

DISC 1　TRACK 20

① あの車は安いです。

②　　　　安いですか？

③ なぜ

④ 彼は今ピアノを練習しています。

⑤　　　　　　3時間

⑥　　　　　　　　　　　　　　しているのですか？

⑦ 私は昨日ピーターに会いました。

⑧　　　　きょうまだ　　　会っていません。

⑨　　　　毎日　　　　　会います。

⑩ 今朝雨が降りました。

⑪ 今朝から　　降っています。

⑫ 明日　　　降るでしょうか？

⑬ あの男の人たちは消防士です。(fireman−firemen)

⑭　　　　　　消防士ですか？

⑮　　　　　　映画が好きですか？

経済的さ

1. That car is cheap.
2. Is that car cheap?
3. Why is that car cheap?
4. He is practicing the piano now.
5. He has been practicing the piano for three hours.
6. Has he been practicing the piano for three hours?
7. I saw Peter yesterday.
8. I haven't seen Peter yet today.
9. I see Peter every day.
10. It rained this morning.
11. It has been raining since this morning.
12. Will it rain tomorrow?
13. Those men are firemen.
14. Are those men firemen?
15. Do those men like movies?

21 快速トレーニング ⑱

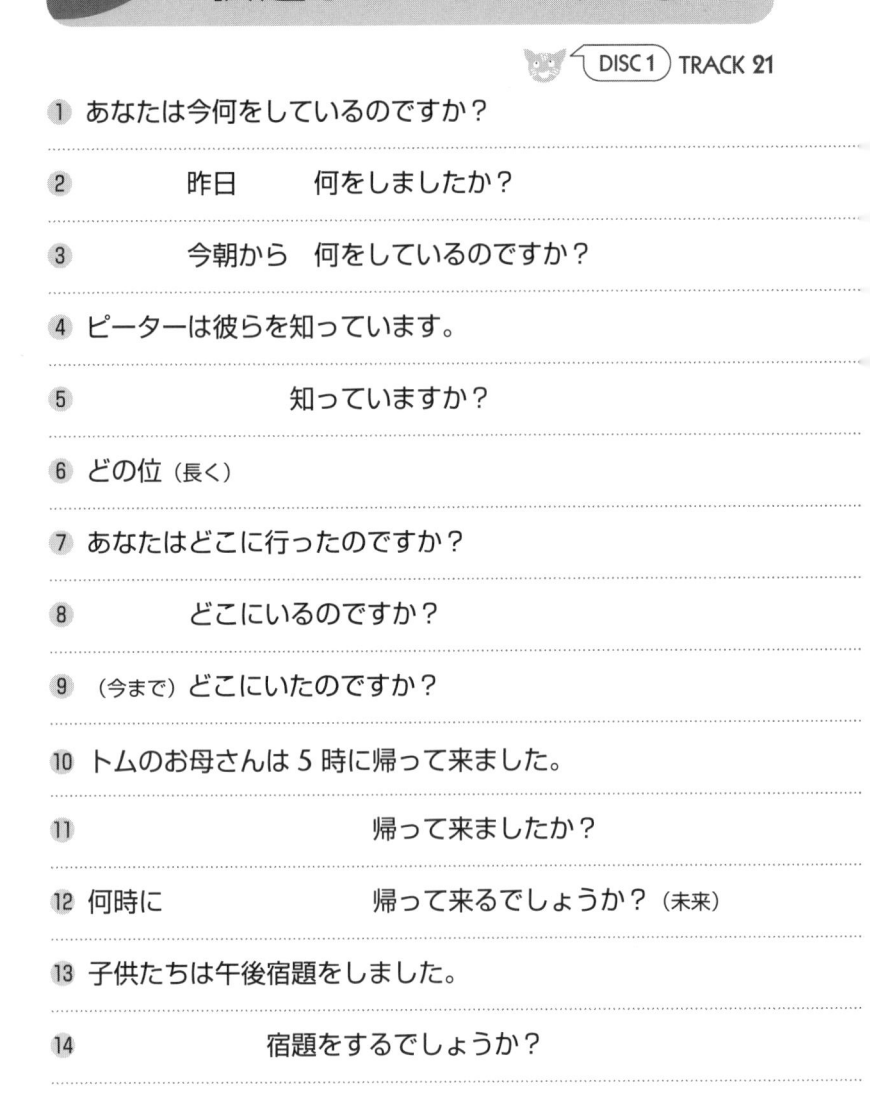

DISC 1　TRACK 21

① あなたは今何をしているのですか？

②　　　昨日　　何をしましたか？

③　　　　今朝から　何をしているのですか？

④ ピーターは彼らを知っています。

⑤　　　　　　知っていますか？

⑥ どの位（長く）

⑦ あなたはどこに行ったのですか？

⑧　　　どこにいるのですか？

⑨ （今まで）どこにいたのですか？

⑩ トムのお母さんは5時に帰って来ました。

⑪　　　　　　　帰って来ましたか？

⑫ 何時に　　　　　帰って来るでしょうか？（未来）

⑬ 子供たちは午後宿題をしました。

⑭　　　宿題をするでしょうか？

⑮　　　もう宿題をしましたか？

1. What are you doing now?

2. What did you do yesterday?

3. What have you been doing since this morning?

4. Peter knows them.

5. Does Peter know them?

6. How long has Peter known them?

7. Where did you go?

8. Where are you?

9. Where have you been?

10. Tom's mother came back at five o'clock.

11. Did Tom's mother come back at five o'clock?

12. What time will Tom's mother come back?

13. The children did their homework in the afternoon.

14. Will the children do their homework in the afternoon?

15. Have the children done their homework yet?

22 快速トレーニング ⑲

1. トムは自分の部屋を掃除しません。
2. 　　　　　　　長い間　　　　　　していません。
3. 　　　　　　　　　　　　　　　していないのですか？
4. ブラウン先生は子供たちに科学 (science) を教えます。
5. 　　　　　　　去年から　　　　　教えています。
6. 誰が
7. メアリーは毎週その町を訪れます。
8. 　　　　　　　先月
9. なぜ　　　　　　　　　　　　訪れたのですか？
10. その少年たちは毎日この公園でサッカーをします。
11. 　　　　　　　　　　　　しますか？
12. いつ
13. 彼女のいとこは3年間パリに住んでいます。
14. 　　　　　　　今　　　　　　住んでいます。
15. どこに

1. Tom doesn't clean his room.

2. Tom hasn't cleaned his room for a long time.

3. Hasn't Tom cleaned his room for a long time?

4. Mr. Brown teaches science to children.

5. Mr. Brown has been teaching science to children since last year.

6. Who has been teaching science to children since last year?

7. Mary visits the town every week.

8. Mary visited the town last month.

9. Why did Mary visit the town last month?

10. The boys play soccer in this park every day.

11. Do the boys play soccer in this park every day?

12. When do the boys play soccer in this park ?

13. Her cousin has lived in Paris for three years.

14. Her cousin lives in Paris now.

15. Where does her cousin live now?

23 快速トレーニング ⑳

DISC 1 TRACK 23

① 彼女は昨夜どこへ行きましたか？

② 明日の午後

③ 空港に行くでしょう。

④ 病院に

⑤ 私の夫は毎日8時に帰宅します。

⑥ 昨夜9時に

⑦ トムは　　　　　帰宅しましたか？

⑧ 何時に

⑨ 毎日帰宅しますか？

⑩ 彼らは

⑪ 学校に行きますか？

⑫ 僕の兄は今中国で暮らしています。

⑬ 3年間

⑭ あなたは　　暮らしているのですか？

⑮ どのくらい

1. Where did she go last night?

2. Where will she go tomorrow afternoon?

3. She will go to the airport tomorrow afternoon.

4. She will go to the hospital tomorrow afternoon.

5. My husband comes home at eight every day.

6. My husband came home at nine last night.

7. Did Tom come home at nine last night?

8. What time did Tom come home last night?

9. What time does Tom come home every day?

10. What time do they come home every day?

11. What time do they go to school every day?

12. My brother lives in China now.

13. My brother has lived in China for three years.

14. Have you lived in Chine for three years?

15. How long have you lived in China?

24 快速トレーニング ㉑

DISC 1 TRACK 24

① 彼女はテーブルの上に卵を１つ置きました。

②　　　　　　　　　　置きましたか？

③ いくつの卵を

④ 何を

⑤ 彼の部屋には多くの本があります。

⑥　　　　　　　　ありますか？

⑦ 冷蔵庫には　たくさんの食べ物

⑧ その学校には　多くの生徒

⑨ 明日のパーティーには　多くの招待客（guest）

⑩ 彼は今図書館にいます。

⑪　　　　　いるのですか？

⑫　　　２時間前

⑬　　　今朝から

⑭ 彼らは

⑮ どのくらい

1. She put an egg on the table.
2. Did she put an egg on the table?
3. How many eggs did she put on the table?
4. What did she put on the table?
5. There are many books in his room.
6. Are there many books in his room?
7. Is there much food in the refrigerator?
8. Are there many students in the school?
9. Will there be many guests at tomorrow's party?
10. He is in the library now.
11. Is he in the library now?
12. Was he in the library two hours ago?
13. Has he been in the library since this morning?
14. Have they been in the library since this morning?
15. How long have they been in the library?

25 快速トレーニング ⑳

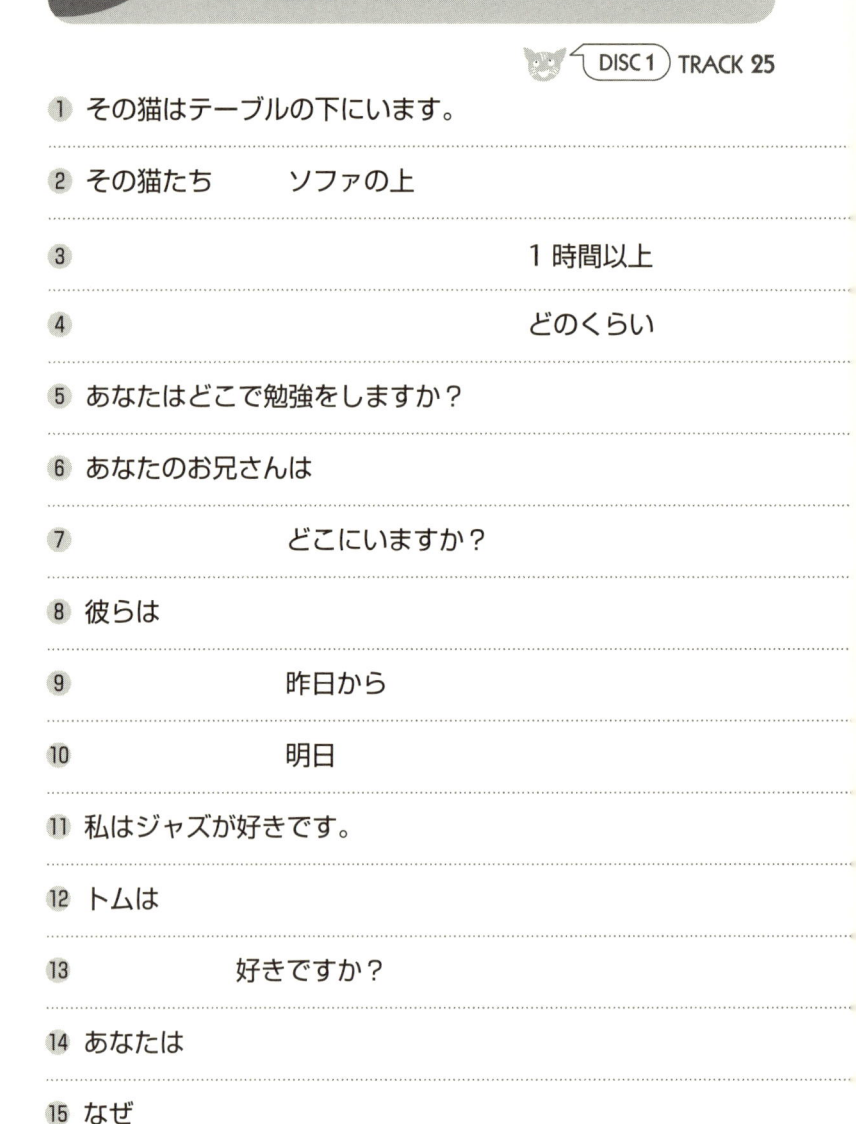

DISC 1 TRACK 25

① その猫はテーブルの下にいます。

② その猫たち　　　ソファの上

③ 　　　　　　　　　　１時間以上

④ 　　　　　　　　　　どのくらい

⑤ あなたはどこで勉強をしますか？

⑥ あなたのお兄さんは

⑦ 　　　　どこにいますか？

⑧ 彼らは

⑨ 　　　　昨日から

⑩ 　　　　明日

⑪ 私はジャズが好きです。

⑫ トムは

⑬ 　　　　好きですか？

⑭ あなたは

⑮ なぜ

1. The cat is under the table.

2. The cats are on the sofa.

3. The cats have been on the sofa for more than an hour.

4. How long have the cats been on the sofa?

5. Where do you study?

6. Where does your brother study?

7. Where is your brother?

8. Where are they?

9. Where have they been since yesterday?

10. Where will they be tomorrow?

11. I like jazz.

12. Tom likes jazz.

13. Does Tom like jazz?

14. Do you like jazz?

15. Why do you like jazz?

26 快速トレーニング ㉓

DISC 1 TRACK 26

① エミリーがこれらの花に水をやります。（水をやる water）

② 　　　　　　　　　やるのですか？

③ 　　　　昨日

④ 　　　　明日

⑤ 誰が

⑥ 私はいつかイタリアに行きます。

⑦ 　　　　去年

⑧ 彼の叔父さんは

⑨ 　　　　　　　行ったのですか？

⑩ 　　　　中国に

⑪ 　　　　　　　　今までに行ったことがありますか？

⑫ 私は毎日朝食に目玉焼き (fried eggs) を食べます。

⑬ あなたのご主人は　　　　　　　食べますか？

⑭ 　　　　　昨日朝食に

⑮ 　　　　何を

1. Emily waters these flowers.

2. Does Emily water these flowers?

3. Did Emily water these flowers yesterday?

4. Will Emily water these flowers tomorrow?

5. Who will water these flowers tomorrow?

6. I will go to Italy some day.

7. I went to Italy last year.

8. His uncle went to Italy last year.

9. Did his uncle go to Italy last year?

10. Did his uncle go to China last year?

11. Has his uncle ever been to China?

12. I eat fried eggs for breakfast every day.

13. Does your husband eat fried eggs for breakfast every day?

14. Did your husband eat fried eggs for breakfast yesterday?

15. What did your husband eat for breakfast yesterday?

27 快速トレーニング ㉔

DISC 1　TRACK 27

1. トムとボブは時々お父さんの車を洗います。

2. 　　　　　　　　　　　　　洗いますか？

3. 　　　　今　　　　　　洗っていますか？

4. 　　　　まだ　　　　　洗っていません。

5. 僕は

6. 私は昨夜流れ星を見ました。（流れ星 falling star）

7. 彼女は　　　見ましたか？

8. 　　　　今までに見たことがありますか？

9. 彼らは　　雪を

10. 　　　　一度も見たことがありません。

11. エミリーは時々、自分の子供たちのためにピアノを弾きます。

12. 　　　　　　　　　　　クッキーを作ります。

13. 　　　　　　　　　　　　作りますか？

14. あなたは

15. 　　　昨日

1. Tom and Bob sometimes wash their father's car.

2. Do Tom and Bob sometimes wash their father's car?

3. Are Tom and Bob washing their father's car now?

4. Tom and Bob haven't washed their father's car yet.

5. I haven't washed my father's car yet.

6. I saw a falling star last night.

7. Did she see a falling star last night?

8. Has she ever seen a falling star?

9. Have they ever seen snow?

10. They have never seen snow.

11. Emily sometimes plays the piano for her children.

12. Emily sometimes makes cookies for her children.

13. Does Emily sometimes make cookies for her children?

14. Do you sometimes make cookies for your children?

15. Did you make cookies for your children yesterday?

28 快速トレーニング ㉕

DISC 1　TRACK 28

① きょうは天気が良いです。

② 昨日は

③ 　　　　　　良かったですか？

④ 　東京では

⑤ 　　雪が降りましたか？

⑥ 　　雨が降りましたか？

⑦ 　　　　　降りませんでした。

⑧ 　　　　1週間降っていません。

⑨ 彼女は昨日日本を発ちました。

⑩ 　　　　もうすぐ　　　　発つでしょう。

⑪ 　　　　　　　　　　到着するでしょう。

⑫ 彼らは　　　　　　　到着するでしょうか？

⑬ 　　　　もう　　　　到着しましたか？

⑭ 　　　　2日前　　　到着しました。

⑮ いつ　　　到着しましたか？

1. It is fine today.

2. It was fine yesterday.

3. Was it fine yesterday?

4. Was it fine in Tokyo yesterday?

5. Did it snow in Tokyo yesterday?

6. Did it rain in Tokyo yesterday?

7. It didn't rain in Tokyo yesterday.

8. It hasn't rained in Tokyo for a week.

9. She left Japan yesterday.

10. She will leave Japan soon.

11. She will arrive in Japan soon.

12. Will they arrive in Japan soon?

13. Have they arrived in Japan yet?

14. They arrived in Japan two days ago.

15. When did they arrive in Japan?

29 快速トレーニング ㉖

DISC 1　TRACK 29

① あなたはりんごをいくつ欲しいのですか？

② ナンシーは

③ 　　　　　　　　食べたのですか？

④ 　　　　　　　　買うでしょうか？（未来）

⑤ 彼らは　本を何冊

⑥ 私は今、自分の部屋で本を読んでいます。

⑦ 彼は

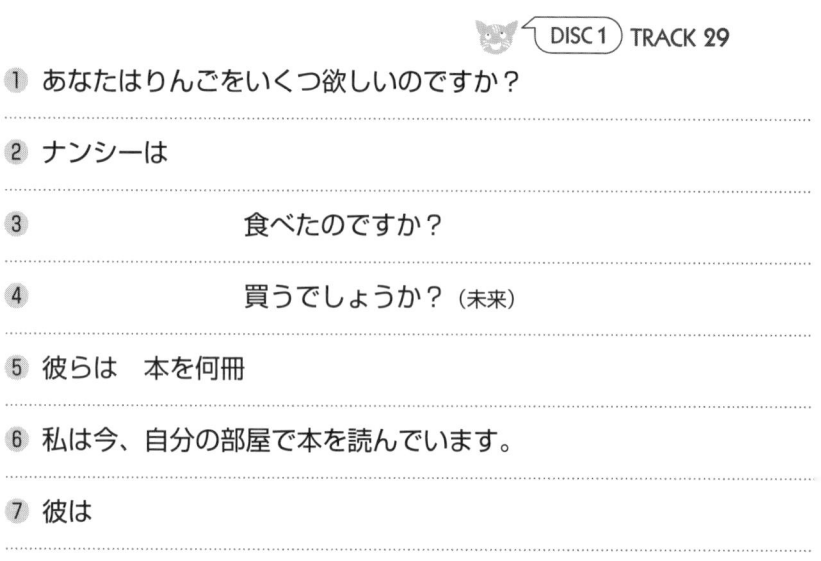

⑧ 　　　3時間　　　　本を読んでいます。

⑨ 　　　　　　　　読んでいるのですか？

⑩ 　　　どのくらい　　読んでいるのですか？

⑪ 私の叔父さんは高校で理科を教えています。（理科 science）

⑫ 　　　　　　　　教えていました。

⑬ 彼女のお母さんは

⑭ 　　　　　　　　教えていましたか？

⑮ 　　　　何を

1. How many apples do you want?
2. How many apples does Nancy want?
3. How many apples did Nancy eat?
4. How many apples will Nancy buy?
5. How many books will they buy?
6. I am reading a book in my room now.
7. He is reading a book in his room now.
8. He has been reading a book in his room for three hours.
9. Has he been reading a book in his room for three hours?
10. How long has he been reading a book in his room?
11. My uncle teaches science at high school.
12. My uncle taught science at high school.
13. Her mother taught science at high school.
14. Did her mother teach science at high school?
15. What did her mother teach at high school?

30 快速トレーニング ㉗

DISC 1　TRACK 30

① トムは、毎日公園でジョギングをします。

②　　　　　　　　　　　　ジョギングをしますか？

③ あの少年たちは

④　　　　　　　今　　　　ジョギングをしていますか？

⑤　　　　　　　　　　　　何をしていますか？

⑥ その男性は私たちに親切でした。

⑦ 彼らは　　　　　彼女に

⑧　　　　　　　　　　　　親切ですか？

⑨　　　　　　　　　　　　厳しいですか？（厳しい strict）

⑩ その先生は

⑪ 私たちはこの家に住んでいます。

⑫ ジョンは

⑬　　　　　　長い間住んでいます。

⑭　　　　　　　　　　住んでいるのですか？

⑮　　　　　どのくらい

1. Tom jogs in the park every day.

2. Does Tom jog in the park every day?

3. Do those boys jog in the park every day?

4. Are those boys jogging in the park now?

5. What are those boys doing in the park now?

6. The man was kind to us.

7. They were kind to her.

8. Are they kind to her?

9. Are they strict with her?

10. Is the teacher strict with her?

11. We live in this house.

12. John lives in this house.

13. John has lived in this house for a long time.

14. Has John lived in this house for a long time?

15. How long has John lived in this house?

31 快速トレーニング ㉘

DISC 1　TRACK 31

1. どちらがあなたの車ですか？

2. 　　　　　　彼の家

3. 　　　　　　彼らの犬

4. どちらの自転車がトムの（もの）ですか？

5. 　　　　　　彼女の（もの）ですか？

6. どちらの人形が

7. どちらのかばんが

8. あの少年は彼女の友達です。

9. 　　　　　　友達ですか？

10. 　　　　彼女を知っていますか？

11. あなたは

12. 彼のお母さんは

13. 　　　　　　彼らを知っています。

14. 　　　　　　　知っていますか？

15. 　　　　彼らに親切ですか？

1. Which is your car?
2. Which is his house?
3. Which is their dog?
4. Which bicycle is Tom's?
5. Which bicycle is hers?
6. Which doll is hers?
7. Which bag is hers?
8. That boy is her friend.
9. Is that boy her friend?
10. Does that boy know her?
11. Do you know her?
12. Does his mother know her?
13. His mother knows them.
14. Does his mother know them?
15. Is his mother kind to them?

アンタのこっちでしょ
返して!

32 快速トレーニング ㉙

DISC 1　TRACK 32

① 私は彼女に毎週会います。

② 彼は

③ 　　　　　　　　　会うのですか？

④ 　　　　　　　（今までに）会ったことがありますか？

⑤ ナンシーは弟に数学を教えます。

⑥ 　　　　　　　　　　　　　教えましたか？

⑦ あなたは

⑧ 　　　　英語を

⑨ 　　　　何を　　　　　　教えましたか？

⑩ あの男の人はエミリーの先生です。

⑪ 　　　　　　　先生ですか？

⑫ 　　　　日本語を話しますか？

⑬ 　　　　何語を話しますか？

⑭ あの人たちは

⑮ 　　　　　　話しているのですか？

1. I see her every week.

2. He sees her every week.

3. Does he see her every week?

4. Has he ever met her?

5. Nancy teaches mathematics to her brother.

6. Did Nancy teach mathematics to her brother?

7. Did you teach mathematics to your brother?

8. Did you teach English to your brother?

9. What did you teach to your brother?

10. That man is Emily's teacher.

11. Is that man Emily's teacher?

12. Does that man speak Japanese?

13. What language does that man speak?

14. What language do those people speak?

15. What language are those people speaking?

33 快速トレーニング ㉚

DISC 1 TRACK 33

① 彼女は若く見える。

② 　　　　　　　　見えますか？

③ 彼らは

④ 　　　　　　強そうに

⑤ 　　　　　　　　　　　　見えませんでした。

⑥ (1杯の) 水を (私に) 持ってきてくれますか？

⑦ 椅子を

⑧ あの本を

⑨ 　　　　　　読んでくれますか？

⑩ 　　　　　　貸してくれますか？

⑪ 　　　　　　本棚に戻してくれますか？

⑫ 彼のお父さんはアメリカにいます。

⑬ 　　　　　　いるのですか？

⑭ 　　　　先週

⑮ 　　　　　　いました。

1. She looks young.

2. Does she look young?

3. Do they look young?

4. Do they look strong?

5. They didn't look strong.

6. Will you please bring me a glass of water?

7. Will you please bring me a chair?

8. Will you please bring me that book?

9. Will you please read me that book?

10. Will you please lend me that book?

11. Will you please put that book back on the bookshelf?

12. His father is in America.

13. Is his father in America?

14. Was his father in America last week?

15. His father was in America last week.

34 快速トレーニング ㉛

DISC 1　TRACK 34

① あれは彼の時計です。

② 　　　　　　　　　　　　ですか？

③ 　　　　彼女のかばん

④ 　　　　　　　　　　　　ではありません。

⑤ 　　　　私たちの間違い

⑥ 　　　　彼らの先生

⑦ あの男の人は

⑧ 　　　　　　　　　　あなたの叔父さんですか？

⑨ トムは動物園に行きました。

⑩ 　　　昨日　　　　　　　行きましたか？

⑪ 　　　　お父さんと一緒に

⑫ あなたは

⑬ 　　　　どこへ

⑭ 　　　　　　あなたのガールフレンドと

⑮ 　　　　来週の日曜

1. That is his watch.

2. Is that his watch?

3. Is that her bag?

4. That isn't her bag.

5. That isn't our mistake.

6. That isn't their teacher.

7. That man isn't their teacher.

8. Is that man your uncle?

9. Tom went to the zoo.

10. Did Tom go to the zoo yesterday?

11. Did Tom go to the zoo with his father yesterday?

12. Did you go to the zoo with your father yesterday?

13. Where did you go with your father yesterday?

14. Where did you go with your girlfriend yesterday?

15. Where will you go with your girlfriend next Sunday?

35 快速トレーニング ㉜

DISC 1 TRACK 35

1 (私が) そこに行きましょうか？

2 　　　本屋に

3 　　　彼に電話しましょうか？

4 　　　夕食を作りましょうか？

5 彼は鋏でその紙を切りました。

6 彼女は　　　　　　　　そのリボンを

7 　　　ナイフで　　そのケーキを

8 　　　　　　　　　　　　切ったのですか？

9 　　　何で

10 彼女はエミリーと一緒に夕食を料理しました。

11 　　　お母さんと一緒に

12 　　　　　　　　　　　　するでしょう。

13 　　　　　　　　　　　　毎日します。

14 　　　あなたと一緒に　　　　　しますか？

15 　　　　　　　　　　　　何をしますか？

1. Shall I go there?
2. Shall I go to the bookstore?
3. Shall I call him?
4. Shall I cook dinner?
5. He cut the paper with scissors.
6. She cut the ribbon with scissors.
7. She cut the cake with a knife.
8. Did she cut the cake with a knife?
9. What did she cut the cake with?
10. She cooked dinner with Emily.
11. She cooked dinner with her mother.
12. She will cook dinner with her mother.
13. She cooks dinner with her mother every day.
14. Does she cook dinner with you every day?
15. What does she do with you every day?

36 快速トレーニング ㉝

DISC 1　TRACK 36

① 私は毎日 3 時間以上テレビを見ます。

② ロバートは

③ 　　　　　　　　　　　　　　見るのですか？

④ 　　　　　　　　5 時間以上　　勉強するのですか？

⑤ あの学生たちは

⑥ 　　　　　なぜ

⑦ エミリーは男の子たちに人気があります。

⑧ 　　　　　　　　人気がありますか？

⑨ 　　　　　　その犬の世話をしますか？

⑩ 　　　　　　　　　　　　します。

⑪ 誰が　　　　　　　　　　　しますか？

⑫ 　　　　　あの部屋を使いますか？

⑬ 　　　　　あの部屋にいますか？

⑭ 　　　　　ドアの後ろに

⑮ 　　　　　庭に

1. I watch TV for more than three hours every day.

2. Robert watches TV for more than three hours every day.

3. Does Robert watch TV for more than three hours every day?

4. Does Robert study for more than five hours every day?

5. Do those students study for more than five hours every day?

6. Why do those students study for more than five hours every day?

7. Emily is popular among boys.

8. Is Emily popular among boys?

9. Does Emily take care of the dog?

10. Emily takes care of the dog.

11. Who takes care of the dog?

12. Who uses that room?

13. Who is in that room?

14. Who is behind the door?

15. Who is in the garden?

37 快速トレーニング ㉞

DISC1 TRACK 37

1. 彼女はその時歌を歌っていました。

2. 　　　　　　　歌っていましたか？

3. その少女たちは

4. 　　　　　今　　　　　教室を掃除しています。

5. 　　　　　1 時間　　　　　しています。

6. 　　　　　昨日　　　　　しました。

7. 誰が　　　　　　　　　しましたか？

8. 私はきょう 4 時に起きました。

9. トムは　　7 時に

10. 　　　　　　　　朝食を食べましたか？

11. あなたは

12. 　　　　　毎日　　　　　食べるのですか？

13. 　　　　　毎日何時に

14. 　　　　　　　　就寝しますか？

15. あなたの息子さんは

1. She was singing a song then.

2. Was she singing a song then?

3. Were the girls singing a song then?

4. The girls are cleaning the classroom now.

5. The girls have been cleaning the classroom for an hour.

6. The girls cleaned the classroom yesterday.

7. Who cleaned the classroom yesterday?

8. I got up at four today.

9. Tom got up at seven today.

10. Did Tom have breakfast at seven today?

11. Did you have breakfast at seven today?

12. Do you have breakfast at seven every day?

13. What time do you have breakfast every day?

14. What time do you go to bed every day?

15. What time does your son go to bed every day?

38 快速トレーニング ㉟

DISC 2 TRACK 01

① 彼はピアニストです。

②　　　　　　ピアニストですか？

③ 彼女のお母さんは

④　　　　　　作家です。

⑤ あの女性の息子さんは

⑥　　　　　　医者になるでしょう。

⑦　　　　　　なるでしょうか？

⑧ 私はメアリーが大好きです。

⑨ 彼の弟は

⑩　　　　　　大好きですか？

⑪　　　　野球が

⑫　　　　　　あまり好きではありません。

⑬ その少年は

⑭　　　　学校が

⑮ その生徒たちは

1. He is a pianist.
2. Is he a pianist?
3. Is her mother a pianist?
4. Her mother is a writer.
5. That woman's son is a writer.
6. That woman's son will be a doctor.
7. Will that woman's son be a doctor?
8. I like Mary a lot.
9. His brother likes Mary a lot.
10. Does his brother like Mary a lot?
11. Does his brother like baseball a lot?
12. His brother doesn't like baseball very much.
13. The boy doesn't like baseball very much.
14. The boy doesn't like school very much.
15. The students don't like school very much.

39 快速トレーニング ㊱

DISC 2 TRACK 02

① あの人たちはドイツ語を話します。

② あの男性は

③ 　　　　　　　　　　何語を話しますか？

④ 　　　　　　　　　　どんな食べ物が好きですか？

⑤ あなたの奥さんは

⑥ トムとロバートは

⑦ 　　　　　　　　　　アメリカ人です。

⑧ 　　　　　　　　　　アメリカ人ですか？

⑨ 　　　　　　　　　　日本語を話しますか？

⑩ あなたは　　　　　　英語を

⑪ あなたのご主人は　　中国語を

⑫ 私の息子は　　　　　　　　話します。

⑬ 　　　　　　　　　　ギリシャ語を勉強しています。

⑭ 　　　　　　大学で　　　　　　勉強しました。

⑮ ナンシーは　　　　　法律を

1. Those people speak German.
2. That man speaks German.
3. What language does that man speak?
4. What food does that man like?
5. What food does your wife like?
6. What food do Tom and Robert like?
7. Tom and Robert are American.
8. Are Tom and Robert American?
9. Do Tom and Robert speak Japanese?
10. Do you speak English?
11. Does your husband speak Chinese?
12. My son speaks Chinese.
13. My son studies Greek.
14. My son studied Greek at college.
15. Nancy studied law at college.

40 快速トレーニング ㊲

DISC 2 TRACK 03

① 私は月に 30 万円稼ぎます。

② 私の妻は　　　　100 万円

③　　　　　　　　　　　　使います。

④ トムは　　　　　　　　使うのですか？

⑤　　　　いくら

⑥　　　　　　先月　　使いましたか？

⑦　　　　　　来月　　使うでしょうか？

⑧ この石鹸はいい香りがする。

⑨　　　いい香りがしますか？

⑩ そのスープは

⑪　　　美味しいですか？（＝いい味がしますか/動詞 taste 使用）

⑫ そのステーキは

⑬　　　美味しかった。

⑭　　　美味しいでしょう。（未来）

⑮　　　美味しくなかった。

1. I earn 300,000 yen a month.

2. My wife earns one million yen a month.

3. My wife spends one million yen a month.

4. Does Tom spend one million yen a month?

5. How much (money) does Tom spend a month?

6. How much (money) did Tom spend last month?

7. How much (money) will Tom spend next month?

8. This soap smells good.

9. Does this soap smell good?

10. Does the soup smell good?

11. Does the soup taste good?

12. Does the steak taste good?

13. The steak tasted good.

14. The steak will taste good.

15. The steak didn't taste good.

41 快速トレーニング ㊳

DISC 2 TRACK 04

① あなたのお父さんは昨日釣りに行ったのですか？

② いつ

③ どこへ

④ 行くのですか？

⑤ ボブは僕の宿題を手伝ってくれた。

⑥ くれるでしょう。

⑦ くれるでしょうか？

⑧ 妹の宿題を 手伝わなかった。

⑨ なぜ 手伝わなかったのですか？

⑩ 彼女は昨日ケーキを焼いた。

⑪ お姉さんと一緒に

⑫ 焼きましたか？

⑬ お母さんの誕生日のために

⑭ 明日 焼くでしょう。

⑮ 焼くでしょうか？

1. Did your father go fishing yesterday?
2. When did your father go fishing ?
3. Where did your father go fishing?
4. Where does your father go fishing?
5. Bob helped me with my homework.
6. Bob will help me with my homework.
7. Will Bob help me with my homework?
8. Bob didn't help his sister with her homework.
9. Why didn't Bob help his sister with her homework?
10. She baked a cake yesterday.
11. She baked a cake with her sister yesterday.
12. Did she bake a cake with her sister yesterday?
13. Did she bake a cake with her sister for their mother's birthday yesterday?
14. She will bake a cake with her sister for their mother's birthday tomorrow.
15. Will she bake a cake with her sister for their mother's birthday tomorrow?

発展編

1 受動態—1

例: He wrote the book. →
　　The book was written by him.

DISC 2　TRACK 05

① Many people know her. →

② Emily loves the cat. →

③ He will invent a new machine. (invent 発明する) →

④ She cleaned the room this morning. →

⑤ The dog bit him. (bite 咬む　活用 bite bit bitten) →

⑥ He composed the song. (compose 作曲する) →

⑦ They will construct a building in front of the station. (construct 建設する) →

⑧ She cut the cake into three pieces. →

⑨ Tom will cook the chicken. →

⑩ Emily teaches them English. →

⑪ Anybody can learn the language. →

⑫ The students respect the professor. →

⑬ Who plays this piano? →

⑭ He will deny the fact. (deny 否定する) →

⑮ My wife chose the house. →

① She is known to many people.

② The cat is loved by Emily.

③ A new machine will be invented by him.

④ The room was cleaned by her this morning.

⑤ He was bitten by the dog.

⑥ The song was composed by him.

⑦ A building will be constructed in front of the station.

⑧ The cake was cut into three pieces by her.

⑨ The chicken will be cooked by Tom.

⑩ They are taught English by Emily. / English is taught to them by Emily.

⑪ The language can be learned by anybody.

⑫ The professor is respected by the students.

⑬ Who is this piano played by? / By whom is this piano played?

⑭ The fact will be denied by him.

⑮ The house was chosen by my wife.

2 受動態—2

DISC 2 TRACK 06

1. Birds eat insects. (insect 昆虫) →
2. The murderer killed five people (murderer 殺人者). →
3. You can't open the door. →
4. The boy broke the window. →
5. They will start a new system. →
6. He will write a novel. →
7. The hen will lay many eggs. →
8. Did she write this letter?→
9. They haven't repaired the car yet. (repair 修理する) →
10. Who takes care of the dog?→
11. He suggested another method. (suggest 提案する method 方法)→
12. The students hate the teacher. →
13. Who cooked the dinner?→
14. Emily didn't forgive him. →
15. He will deal with the matter. (deal with~~を扱う、処理する matter 事柄・件)→

1. Insects are eaten by birds.
2. Five people were killed by the murderer.
3. The door can't be opened.
4. The window was broken by the boy.
5. A new system will be started.
6. A novel will be written by him.
7. Many eggs will be laid by the hen.
8. Was this letter written by her?
9. The car hasn't been repaired yet.
10. By whom is the dog taken care of? / Who is the dog taken care of by?
11. Another method was suggested by him.
12. The teacher is hated by the students.
13. Who was the dinner cooked by? / By whom was the dinner cooked?
14. He wasn't forgiven by Emily.
15. The matter will be dealt with by him.

3 受動態—3

DISC 2　TRACK 07

① The girl sang an old song. →

② The boy picked up the stone. →

③ The gardener will trim the tree. (gardener 庭師 trim 剪定する)→

④ Who runs this restaurant? (run 経営する) →

⑤ The guests use this phone. →

⑥ A girl smiled at me. →

⑦ The man wrote a sentence with a pencil. →

⑧ Who will raise the child? (raise 育てる) →

⑨ The scientist solved the problem. (solve 解く) →

⑩ Who has caused the accident?→

⑪ The woman sweeps the floors every day. (sweep 掃く)

⑫ Who put out the fire? (put out 消す) →

⑬ He has turned off the lights. →

⑭ The waitress cleared the table. (clear 〜の上のものをどかして片付ける)→

⑮ You must keep the door shut. →

郵便はがき

料金受取人払郵便

牛込局承認
6356

差出有効期間
2026年12月31日
まで

（切手不要）

162-8790

東京都新宿区
岩戸町12レベッカビル
ベレ出版

　　読者カード係　行

お名前		年齢
ご住所　〒		
電話番号	性別	ご職業
メールアドレス		

個人情報は小社の読者サービス向上のために活用させていただきます。

ご購読ありがとうございました。ご意見、ご感想をお聞かせください。

● **ご購入された書籍**

● **ご意見、ご感想**

● 図書目録の送付を　　　　　　　☐ 希望する　　☐ 希望しない

ご協力ありがとうございました。
小社の新刊などの情報が届くメールマガジンをご希望される方は、
小社ホームページ（https://www.beret.co.jp/）からご登録くださいませ。

1. An old song was sung by the girl.

2. The stone was picked up by the boy.

3. The tree will be trimmed by the gardener.

4. Who is this restaurant run by? / By whom is this restaurant run?

5. This phone is used by the guests.

6. I was smiled at by a girl.

7. A sentence was written with a pencil by the man.

8. Who will the child be raised by? / By whom will the child be raised?

9. The problem was solved by the scientist.

10. Who has the accident been caused by? / By whom has the accident been caused?

11. The floors are swept every day by the woman.

12. Who was the fire put out by? / By whom was the fire put out?

13. The lights have been turned off by him.

14. The table was cleared by the waitress.

15. The door must be kept shut.

4 受動態―4

1. Who has eaten the cake?→
2. The children pulled the rope. →
3. The millionaire bought the house. (millionaire＝百万長者、大金持ち)→
4. The vet put the dog to sleep. (vet＝獣医 put~to sleep~を安楽死させる)
5. Who will build the house?→
6. His wife made a cup of coffee. →
7. Who turned on the TV?→
8. She and her daughter prepared the party. (prepare~を準備する) →
9. Has he fixed the car yet? (fix 修理する) →
10. She didn't return the book to the bookshelf. →
11. Did Tom kick the ball?→
12. The students will tear down the notice. (tear down 破る notice 告知)→
13. He loosened the lid of the bottle. (lid 蓋 loosen ゆるめる)→
14. He set the slaves free. (set~free を自由にする) →
15. Nobody can find the place. →

① Who has the cake been eaten by? / By whom has the cake been eaten?

② The rope was pulled by the children.

③ The house was bought by the millionaire.

④ The dog was put to sleep by the vet.

⑤ Who will the house be built by? / By whom will the house be built?

⑥ A cup of coffee was made by his wife.

⑦ Who was the TV turned on by? / By whom was the TV turned on?

⑧ The party was prepared by her and her daughter.

⑨ Has the car been fixed by him yet?

⑩ The book wasn't returned to the bookshelf by her.

⑪ Was the ball kicked by Tom?

⑫ The notice will be torn down by the students.

⑬ The lid of the bottle was loosened by him.

⑭ The slaves were set free by him.

⑮ The place can be found by nobody.

5

must、can't (はずがない)、may

DISC 2 TRACK 09

① 彼は毎日部屋を掃除しなければなりません。

② 　　　英語を勉強しなければ

③ 　　　怒っているに違いありません。

④ 　　　お金持ちに違いありません。

⑤ 　　　お金持ちのはずがありません。

⑥ 　　　そこにいるはずがありません。

⑦ 私は部屋に入ってもいいですか？

⑧ 　　　家に帰ってもいいですか？

⑨ 彼女は帰ってくるかもしれません。

⑩ 　　　幸福かもしれません。

⑪ 　　　彼と結婚するかもしれません。

⑫ 　　　天才 (a genius) かもしれません。

1. He must clean the room every day.
2. He must study English every day.
3. He must be angry.
4. He must be rich.
5. He can't be rich.
6. He can't be there.
7. May I go into the room?
8. May I go home?
9. She may (might) come back.
10. She may (might) be happy.
11. She may (might) marry him.
12. She may (might) be a genius.

あなたはネズミが
好きにな〜る
そして
結婚したくな〜る

6. have to、be going to、be able to

DISC 2 TRACK 10

1. 私は彼らと会わなければならない。

2. 彼は

3. 　　　　　　　　もっと勉強しなければなりません。

4. 　　　　　　　　罰されなければなりません。（罰する punish）

5. 私は来月日本を発つ予定です。

6. 彼女は　　　　　　予定なのですか？

7. 　　　日本に来る

8. 　　　彼と結婚する

9. 彼はロシア語 (Russian) を話せるようになるでしょう。

10. 　　　　　　　　を話せました。

11. 彼は落ち着いていられるでしょうか？（落ち着いている＝stay calm）

12. 　　落ち着いていられました。

世界は広い！
旅立ちの時ですぞ
ドブネズミ君！

ただのネズミです

1. I have to meet them.

2. He has to meet them.

3. He has to study more.

4. He has to be punished.

5. I'm going to leave Japan next month.

6. Is she going to leave Japan next month?

7. Is she going to come to Japan next month?

8. Is she going to marry him next month?

9. He will be able to speak Russian.

10. He was able to speak Russian.

11. Will he be able to stay calm?

12. He was able to stay calm.

7 不定詞—1 名詞的用法

DISC 2 TRACK 11

① 私は彼女に会いたいです。

② 彼は

③ 　　　　　アメリカに行きたがっています。

④ 　　　　　　　　行きたがっていますか？

⑤ 彼女はピアノを弾き始めました。

⑥ 　　宿題をし始めました。

⑦ 　　　　　もうし始めましたか？（現在完了）

⑧ 私はその車を買うことを決めました。

⑨ 彼は　　　　　　決めるでしょう。（未来）

⑩ 彼らは　　　　　まだ決めていません。（現在完了）

⑪ 彼女はフランス語を習いたがっています。

⑫ 　　長い間　　　習いたがっています。（現在完了）

1. I want to meet her.

2. He wants to meet her.

3. He wants to go to America.

4. Does he want to go to America?

5. She began to play the piano.

6. She began to do her homework.

7. Has she begun to do her homework yet?

8. I decided to buy the car.

9. He will decide to buy the car.

10. They haven't decided to buy the car yet.

11. She wants to learn French.

12. She has wanted to learn French for a long time.

8 不定詞—2 形容詞的用法

DISC 2 TRACK 12

① 僕にはきょうしなければならないこと (するべき何か) があります。

② あなたには　　　　　　　　ありますか？

③ 彼には　　　　　　　　　　何もない。

④ 彼女は　　　　　　　　　　なかった。

⑤ 　　飲み物 (飲むための何か) が　欲しかった。

⑥ あなたは　　　　　　　　　欲しいですか？

⑦ 僕には君に言うことがあります。(言うべき何かを持っている)

⑧ 　　彼に見せるものが

⑨ 　　彼にあげるものを　　買った。

⑩ 彼はお母さんに送る手紙を書くつもりです。

⑪ 　　　　　　　　　　　　書いています。

⑫ 　　妻に送る手紙　　　書いたところです。(現在完了)

1. I have something to do today.

2. Do you have anything to do today?

3. He has nothing to do today. / He doesn't have anything to do today.

4. She had nothing to do today. / She didn't have anything to do today.

5. She wanted something to drink.

6. Do you want anything (something) to drink?

7. I have something to tell you.

8. I have something to show him.

9. I bought something to give him.

10. He is going to write a letter to send to his mother.

11. He is writing a letter to send to his mother.

12. He has written a letter to send to his wife.

お母さんへ
どうかおこづかいを
あげて下さい

9 不定詞—3 副詞的用法（目的）

DISC 2 TRACK 13

① 彼は雑誌を買いに本屋に行きました。

② 　　辞書を買いに　　　　　　行ったのですか？

③ 　　美術を勉強しに　　フランスへ

④ 多くの人が　　　　　　　　　行きます。

⑤ 　　痩せる (lose weight) ために　ジョギングをします。

⑥ あなたは　　　　　　　　　　しているのですか？（進行形）

⑦ 　　　　　　　　　　　　何をしましたか？

⑧ トムは　大金を稼ぐ (earn) ために

⑨ 　　　　　　　　　懸命に (hard) 働きました。

⑩ 　　　家族を養うために　働いています。（進行形）

⑪ 　　　　　　　仕事を変える (change jobs) でしょう。

⑫ あなたは　　　　　　　　変えたのですか？

1. He went to the bookstore to buy a magazine.

2. Did he go to the bookstore to buy a dictionary?

3. Did he go to France to study art?

4. Many people go to France to study art.

5. Many people jog to lose weight.

6. Are you jogging to lose weight?

7. What did you do to lose weight?

8. What did Tom do to earn a lot of money?

9. Tom worked hard to earn a lot of money.

10. Tom is working hard to support his family.

11. Tom will change jobs to support his family.

12. Did you change jobs to support your family?

10 不定詞—4 副詞的用法（感情の原因）

DISC 2 TRACK 14

① 彼女は彼に会って喜んだ（happy）。

② 　　　あなたに会って　　　　喜びましたか？

③ あなたのおばあさんは

④ 　　あなたの手紙を受取って（receive）　喜ぶでしょう。（未来）

⑤ あなたのご両親は　読んで

⑥ 彼らは　　　　　　　　　　驚いた。

⑦ 　その結果（result）を知って　がっかりした（disappointed）。

⑧ 　　　　　　　　　　　　　　がっかりするでしょうか？

⑨ 彼女は　　　　　　　　　　がっかりしなかった。

⑩ 　　　　　　　　　　　　　　がっかりした。

⑪ エミリーは　　　　　　　　ショックを受けた（shocked）。

⑫ 　　　その事故を見て

1. She was happy to see him.

2. Was she happy to see you?

3. Was your grandmother happy to see you?

4. Your grandmother will be happy to receive your letter.

5. Your parents will be happy to read your letter.

6. They were surprised to read your letter.

7. They were disappointed to know the result.

8. Will they be disappointed to know the result?

9. She wasn't disappointed to know the result.

10. She was disappointed to know the result.

11. Emily was shocked to know the result.

12. Emily was shocked to see the accident.

11 動名詞―1 目的語

DISC 2 TRACK 15

① 彼は野球をするのが好きです。

② 私は　　　　ピアノを弾くのが

③ 彼女は　　　　　　　　好きですか？

④ 　　　　　　　　　　好きではありません。

⑤ エミリーは歴史を勉強するのを楽しみます。

⑥ 　　　　　　　　　　楽しみますか？

⑦ 　　テニスをするのを

⑧ 　　　　　　　　　　終えました。

⑨ あなたはもうすぐその本を読み終えますか？（未来）

⑩ 　　　　　　もう　　終えましたか？（現在完了）

⑪ 私は　　　　まだ　　終えていません。

⑫ 　　　　　　昨日　　終えました。

1. He likes playing baseball.
2. I like playing the piano.
3. Does she like playing the piano?
4. She doesn't like playing the piano.
5. Emily enjoys studying history.
6. Does Emily enjoy studying history?
7. Does Emily enjoy playing tennis?
8. Emily finished playing tennis.
9. Will you finish reading the book soon?
10. Have you finished reading the book yet?
11. I haven't finished reading the book yet.
12. I finished reading the book yesterday.

12 動名詞—2 主語

DISC 2 TRACK 16

① 外国語を勉強するのは面白い。

② 　　　　　　　　　　難しい。

③ ピアノを弾くのは

④ 　　　　　　　　　　楽しい (fun) ですか？

⑤ そこで暮らすことは

⑥ 本を読むことは

⑦ 多くの本を読むことは大変 (tough) でしょう。(未来)

⑧ 　　　　　　　　　　でしょうか？

⑨ 我慢強い (patient) ことが大切です。

⑩ 　　　　　　　　　　大切ですか？

⑪ 他人に (to others) 親切であることは

⑫ 　　　　　　　　　　大変 (hard) です。

1. Studying foreign languages is interesting.

2. Studying foreign languages is difficult.

3. Playing the piano is difficult.

4. Is playing the piano fun?

5. Is living there fun?

6. Is reading books fun?

7. Reading many books will be tough.

8. Will reading many books be tough?

9. Being patient is important.

10. Is being patient important?

11. Is being kind to others important?

12. Being kind to others is hard.

13 比較—1

DISC 2 TRACK 17

① トムはボブと同じくらいの背丈です。

②　　　　　同じ年齢ですか？

③　　　　　同じくらい上手に日本語を話します。

④ エミリーはその女の子たちの中で一番可愛い。

⑤　　　　　　　　一番早く走る。

⑥　　　　　　　　一番知的 (intelligent) です。

⑦ 彼はあなたと同じくらい有名になるでしょう。

⑧　　　　　有名になるでしょうか？

⑨　　あなたより　　　有名に

⑩ あなたはコーヒーと紅茶ではどちらの方が好きですか？

⑪　　　　　犬と猫では

⑫ あなたのお母さんは

1. Tom is as tall as Bob.

2. Is Tom as old as Bob?

3. Tom speaks Japanese as well as Bob.

4. Emily is the prettiest of the girls.

5. Emily runs the fastest of the girls.

6. Emily is the most intelligent of the girls.

7. He will be as famous as you.

8. Will he be as famous as you?

9. Will he be more famous than you?

10. Which do you like better, tea or coffee?

11. Which do you like better, dogs or cats?

12. Which does your mother like better, dogs or cats?

14 比較—2

DISC 2 TRACK 18

① きょうは昨日と同じくらい暑いです。

② 　　　　　昨日ほど暑くないです。

③ 　　　　　昨日より暑いです。

④ 　　　　　昨日より暑くなるでしょうか？

⑤ ロバートはビルと同じくらいのお金を持っています。

⑥ 　　　　　同じくらいの本を

⑦ 　　　　　ビルよりたくさんの本を

⑧ 彼女はメアリーよりずっと疲れていました。

⑨ 　　　　　　　ずっと人気がありました。

⑩ 　　　　クラスで一番人気がありました。

⑪ 彼の妻は町の他のどの女性よりも美しい。

⑫ 　　　　町の他のどの女性よりも料理が上手い。

1. Today it is as hot as yesterday.

2. Today it isn't as hot as yesterday.

3. It is hotter today than yesterday.

4. Will it be hotter today than yesterday?

5. Robert has as much money as Bill does.

6. Robert has as many books as Bill does.

7. Robert has more books than Bill.

8. She was much more tired than Mary.

9. She was much more popular than Mary.

10. She was the most popular in the class.

11. His wife is more beautiful than any other woman in town.

12. His wife cooks better than any other woman in town.

15　SVO＋to 不定詞
—1 want

DISC 2　TRACK 19

① 私はあなたにここに来て欲しい。

② もっと勉強して欲しい。

③ 野菜を食べて欲しい。

④ 静かにして欲しい。

⑤ あなたは私に（あなたを）手伝って欲しいのですか？

⑥ 彼らに親切にして欲しいのですか？

⑦ あなたと一緒にいて欲しいのですか？

⑧ 日本語を話して欲しいのですか？

⑨ 彼女は彼に煙草を吸って欲しくない。

⑩ あの女性と話して欲しくない。

⑪ 外国に行って欲しくない。

⑫ その話をして欲しくない。

1. I want you to come here.

2. I want you to study more.

3. I want you to eat vegetables.

4. I want you to be quiet.

5. Do you want me to help you?

6. Do you want me to be kind to them?

7. Do you want me to be with you?

8. Do you want me to speak Japanese?

9. She doesn't want him to smoke cigarettes.

10. She doesn't want him to talk to that woman.

11. She doesn't want him to go abroad.

12. She doesn't want him to tell the story.

16 SVO＋to 不定詞—2 ask

DISC 2 TRACK 20

① 私は彼女に手伝ってくれるように頼んだ。

② 　　　　　　朝食を作ってくれるように

③ 　　　　　　静かにするように

④ 　　　　　　宿題を手伝うように

⑤ 　　　　　　ここに帰ってくるように

⑥ あなたは彼に働くように頼みましたか？

⑦ 　　　　　　車を洗うように

⑧ 　　　　　　ドアを閉めるように

⑨ 　　　　　　部屋を掃除するように

⑩ 彼は私にこの仕事をしてくれとは頼みませんでした。

⑪ 　　　　　　彼を手伝ってくれとは

⑫ 　　　　　　彼の助手になってくれとは

1. I asked her to help me.
2. I asked her to cook breakfast.
3. I asked her to be quiet.
4. I asked her to help me with my homework.
5. I asked her to come back here.
6. Did you ask him to work?
7. Did you ask him to wash the car?
8. Did you ask him to close the door?
9. Did you ask him to clean the room?
10. He didn't ask me to do this job.
11. He didn't ask me to help him.
12. He didn't ask me to be his assistant.

17 SVO ＋ to 不定詞 —3 tell

DISC 2 TRACK 21

① 私は彼女にピアノの練習をするように言いました。

② 歌を歌うように

③ 注意深くなるように

④ そこへ行くように

⑤ 彼はあなたに彼女と会うように言いましたか？

⑥ 彼と働く

⑦ 社交的になるように（sociable）

⑧ 彼の宿題を手伝う

⑨ トムは私たちに皿を洗うように言わなかった。

⑩ 窓を開けるように

⑪ もっと早く帰宅するように

⑫ 毎日ここへ来るように

1. I told her to practice the piano.
2. I told her to sing.
3. I told her to be careful.
4. I told her to go there.
5. Did he tell you to meet her?
6. Did he tell you to work with him?
7. Did he tell you to be sociable?
8. Did he tell you to help him with his homework?
9. Tom didn't tell us to wash the dishes.
10. Tom didn't tell us to open the window.
11. Tom didn't tell us to come home earlier.
12. Tom didn't tell us to come here every day.

18 that 節—1

DISC 2 TRACK 22

① 私は、彼は正直だと思います。

② 　　　彼はハンサム (good-looking) だと

③ 　　　　　　　　　　あなたは思いましたか？

④ あなたは彼がアメリカ人だと信じていますか？

⑤ 　　　この話が本当であると

⑥ 私は　　　　　　　　　信じます。

⑦ 　　　彼らが約束を守ると (keep one's promise) (未来)

⑧ 彼は彼女が帰ってくることを望んでいます。

⑨ 　　　明日晴れることを

⑩ あなたは　　　　　　　望んでいますか？

⑪ 彼女は彼が一度もその国に行ったことがないことを知っています。

⑫ 　　　彼が医師になりたいことを

1. I think that he is honest.
2. I think that he is good-looking.
3. Did you think that he was good-looking?
4. Do you believe that he is American?
5. Do you believe that this story is true?
6. I believe that this story is true.
7. I believe that they will keep their promise.
8. He hopes that she will come back.
9. He hopes that it will be fine tomorrow.
10. Do you hope that it will be fine tomorrow?
11. She knows that he has never been to the country.
12. She knows that he wants to be a doctor.

19 that 節—2

① 彼女は、彼が自分を避けていると感じている。

② 　　　夫に深く愛されていると

③ 　　　その問題はもう一方より重要であると

④ 彼らは、その言語を学ぶことは難しいということがわかる (find) でしょう。

⑤ 　　　この方法 (method) が一番良いということが

⑥ 　　　その男性がとても賢い (wise) ということが

⑦ 私は、彼らはきっと結婚すると思う。(きっと〜だと思う＝be sure)

⑧ 　　　彼らはもう出発してしまったと

⑨ 　　　彼女はその試験に受かると

⑩ 私はあなたがその試験に受かって嬉しい (glad)。

⑪ 　　　彼女が私のプレゼントを気に入ってくれて

⑫ 　　　彼が良い仕事について (get a good job)

1. She feels that he is avoiding her.

2. She feels that she is loved deeply by her husband.

3. She feels that the problem is more important than the other.

4. They will find that learning the language is difficult.

5. They will find that this method is the best.

6. They will find that the man is very wise.

7. I'm sure that they will get married.

8. I'm sure that they have already left.

9. I'm sure that she will pass the exam.

10. I'm glad that you passed the exam.

11. I'm glad that she liked my present.

12. I'm glad that he got a good job.

あ、ありがと…

僕がつかまえて
僕が作ったの

20 間接疑問文―1

DISC 2 TRACK 24

① 私は彼がどこで生まれたのか知りません。

② 　　彼がいつ帰ってくるのか

③ 　　　　　　　　　　　　　あなたは知っていますか？

④ 彼が夕食に何を食べたのか

⑤ あなたが何をしたいのか私に教えてください。

⑥ 　　　どうやって英語を勉強したのか

⑦ 　　　なぜ日本語を勉強しているのか

⑧ 彼女は、彼が昨日何をしたか知っています。

⑨ 　　　その時何をしていたか

⑩ 　　　どのくらい彼が日本に住んでいるか

⑪ 私は彼が月にどのくらいのお金を稼ぐのか知りたいです。(稼ぐ earn)

⑫ 　　　いつこの町に来たのか

1. I don't know where he was born.

2. I don't know when he will come back.

3. Do you know when he will come back?

4. Do you know what he had (ate) for dinner?

5. Please tell me what you want to do.

6. Please tell me how you studied English.

7. Please tell me why you are studying Japanese.

8. She knows what he did yesterday.

9. She knows what he was doing then.

10. She knows how long he has lived in Japan.

11. I want to know how much money he earns a month.

12. I want to know when he came to this town.

21 間接疑問文—2

DISC 2 TRACK 25

① 私は、彼が明日来るのかわかりません。

② 　　　明日晴れるのか

③ 　　　彼女が彼を好きなのか

④ あなたは彼が英語を話すか知っていますか？

⑤ 　　　　　日本に行ったことがあるか

⑥ 彼女は彼が結婚しているのか知らない。

⑦ 　　　彼がまだアメリカにいるのか

⑧ 　　　トムが彼らに会いたがっているのか

⑨ 　　　この話が本当なのか

⑩ 彼らがこの町に住んでいるのか教えてくれますか？

⑪ 彼女が来週彼らと会う予定なのか

⑫ 彼女がもうすでにそこに着いたのかどうか

1. I don't know if he will come tomorrow.

2. I don't know if it will be fine tomorrow.

3. I don't know if she likes him.

4. Do you know if he speaks English?

5. Do you know if he has ever been to Japan?

6. She doesn't know if he is married.

7. She doesn't know if he is still in America.

8. She doesn't know if Tom wants to see them.

9. She doesn't know if this story is true.

10. Will you please tell me if they live in this town?

11. Will you please tell me if she is going to meet them next week?

12. Will you please tell me if she has already arrived there?

22 従属節—1

① 彼が朝起きた時、晴れていた。

② 　　家を出た時、

③ 　　　　　　　　雨が降っていましたか？

④ 彼が帰って来た時、奥さんは夕食を料理していました。

⑤ 彼が犬と散歩をしていた時、

⑥ 　　　　　　　　　　　奥さんは何をしていましたか？

⑦ 明日晴れたら、僕は釣りに行きます。

⑧ 　雨だったら　　　行きません。

⑨ 君が僕に家にいて欲しいなら

⑩ お金持ちになったら、私はその家を買うでしょう。

⑪ 結婚したら

⑫ 妻が (それを) 気に入ったら、

1. When he got up in the morning, it was fine.

2. When he left home, it was fine.

3. Was it raining when he left home?

4. When he came home, his wife was cooking dinner.

5. While he was taking a walk with his dog, his wife was cooking dinner.

6. What was his wife doing while he was taking a walk with his dog?

7. If it is fine tomorrow, I will go fishing.

8. If it is rainy tomorrow, I won't go fishing.

9. If you want me to be at home, I won't go fishing.

10. If I become rich, I will buy the house.

11. If I get married, I will buy the house.

12. If my wife likes it, I will buy the house.

23 従属節—2

DISC 2 TRACK 27

① サッカーの試合を見たかったので、彼は家に早く帰った。

② 何もすることがなかったので、

③ 疲れていたので

④ 疲れていたけれど、彼は働くのを止めなかった。

⑤ お金持ちになったけれど、

⑥ お金持ちになった後、彼は世界中を旅行した。

⑦ 大学を卒業した後、

⑧ 大学を卒業する前に、

⑨ 　　　　　　　　　　　　　するでしょう。

⑩ この仕事を終えるまで、私は出かけることができません。

⑪ 両親が帰宅するまで、

⑫ 　　　　　　彼女は家にいた。

① As (Since) he wanted to see the soccer game, he went home early. /
He went home early because he wanted to see the soccer game.

② As (Since) he had nothing to do, he went home early. /
He went home early because he had nothing to do.

③ As (Since) he was tired, he went home early. /
He went home early because he was tired.

④ Although (Though) he was tired, he didn't stop working.

⑤ Although (Though) he became rich, he didn't stop working.

⑥ After he became rich, he traveled around the world.

⑦ After he graduated from college, he traveled around the world.

⑧ Before he graduated from college, he traveled around the world.

⑨ Before he graduates from college, he will travel around the world.

⑩ I can't go out until (till) I finish this work.

⑪ I can't go out until (till) my parents come home.

⑫ She stayed at home until (till) her parents came home.

24 分詞—1

① 走っている少年たちは、彼の生徒です。

② 公園で走っている少年たちは

③ 　　　サッカーをしている

④ 　　　　　　　　　　　　彼の生徒ですか？

⑤ その割れた窓はいつ直されるのでしょうか？（直す repair）

⑥ トムに割られた窓は

⑦ 　　　　　　もう直されました。

⑧ みんながその眠っている赤ちゃんを見つめていた。

⑨ 　　　ゆりかご（揺りかご cradle）で眠っている赤ちゃんを

⑩ 　　　ピカソ（Picasso）に描かれた絵を

⑪ その男は吠えている犬に石を投げつけた。

⑫ 　　　自分に向って吠えている犬に

1. The running boys are his students.

2. The boys running in the park are his students.

3. The boys playing soccer in the park are his students.

4. Are the boys playing soccer in the park his students?

5. When will the broken window be repaired?

6. When will the window broken by Tom be repaired?

7. The window broken by Tom has already been repaired.

8. Everyone was looking at the sleeping baby.

9. Everyone was looking at the baby sleeping in the cradle.

10. Everyone was looking at the picture painted by Picasso.

11. The man threw a stone at the barking dog.

12. The man threw a stone at the dog barking at him.

25 分詞—2

DISC 2 TRACK 29

1. ほほえんでいるあの男性を見なさい。

2. 私たちにほほえんでいるあの男性を

3. 彼らは傷ついた人たちを助けた。（傷つける injure）

4. 　　　その事故で傷ついた人たちを

5. あそこに立っている男の人は、ブラウンさんです。

6. ナンシーと話している男の人は

7. 　　　　　　　　　　　ブラウンさんですか？

8. 彼女にはその会社で働いているおじさんがいます。

9. 　　　大学で経済学（economics）を教えているおじさん

10. 　　　インド（India）に住んでいる

11. 知事に選出されたその男性は、彼の友人です。（選出する elect）

12. このホテルを経営している男性は、（経営する run）

1. Look at that smiling man.
2. Look at that man smiling at us.
3. They helped the injured people.
4. They helped the people injured in the accident.
5. The man standing there is Mr. Brown.
6. The man talking to Nancy is Mr. Brown.
7. Is the man talking to Nancy Mr. Brown?
8. She has an uncle working in the company.
9. She has an uncle teaching economics at college.
10. She has an uncle living in India.
11. The man elected governor is his friend.
12. The man running this hotel is his friend.

26 関係代名詞—1 (文から関係代名詞節への変換—1)

例: The man lives in the big house.→
the man <u>who (that) lives in the big house</u>

DISC 2 TRACK 30

1. The scientist made a great discovery. →the scientist〜

2. She bought the dress yesterday. →the dress〜

3. The man's wife was born in Japan. →the man〜

4. I met an attractive lady at the party. →the attractive lady〜

5. The writer wrote a wonderful novel. →the writer〜

6. The journalist wrote the article for the magazine. →the article〜

7. The man's name is known to everybody. →the man〜

8. The young man saved the child from drowning. →the young man〜

9. The magazine is very popular among young women. →the magazine〜

10. I made a chair with my father last Sunday. →the chair〜

11. The girl's mother is a famous singer. →the girl〜

12. His uncle took the picture last year. →the picture〜

1. the scientist who (that) made a great discovery

2. the dress (which / that) she bought yesterday

3. the man whose wife was born in Japan

4. the attractive lady (whom / that) I met at the party

5. the writer who (that) wrote a wonderful novel

6. the article (which / that) the journalist wrote for the magazine

7. the man whose name is known to everybody

8. the young man who (that) saved the child from drowning

9. the magazine which (that) is very popular among young women

10. the chair (which / that) I made with my father last Sunday

11. the girl whose mother is a famous singer

12. the picture (which / that) his uncle took last year

27 関係代名詞—2 (文から関係代名詞節への変換—2)

DISC 2 TRACK 31

① The man invented a very useful machine. →the man〜

② I have known the woman for twenty years. →the woman〜

③ The building was destroyed by the earthquake. →the building〜

④ The boy's father runs many restaurants. →the boy〜

⑤ She loved the man from the bottom of her heart.
→the man〜

⑥ The boy likes soccer better than anything else. →the boy〜

⑦ They used the tool to build their house. →the tool〜

⑧ The man smokes more than sixty cigarettes a day.
→the man〜

⑨ Tom painted the walls yellow yesterday. →the walls〜

⑩ I taught the woman's son English last year. →the woman〜

⑪ They are going to buy the big house next year. →the big house〜

⑫ The teacher encouraged me to go up to college.
→the teacher〜

1. the man who (that) invented a very useful machine

2. the woman (whom / that) I have known for twenty years

3. the building which (that) was destroyed by the earthquake

4. the boy whose father runs many restaurants

5. the man (whom / that) she loved from the bottom of her heart

6. the boy who (that) likes soccer better than anything else

7. the tool (which / that) they used to build their house

8. the man who (that) smokes more than sixty cigarettes a day

9. the walls (which / that) Tom painted yellow yesterday

10. the woman whose son I taught English last year

11. the big house (which / that) they are going to buy next year

12. the teacher who (that) encouraged me to go up to college

28 関係代名詞—3

DISC 2 TRACK 32

1. 彼女が買った家はとても大きい。

2. 彼らが建てた家は

3. 　　　　　　　　　　美しい

4. 　　　　　　　　　　美しいですか？

5. 彼が結婚した女性は

6. 　　　　　　　　　　アメリカ人です。

7. その小説を書いた作家は

8. 彼が私に紹介してくれたその男性は

9. 彼らは、彼が私に紹介してくれたその男性を知っていますか？

10. 彼らは　　　　　　　　　　　　知りません。

11. 　　　　　　　　　　　　　　　尊敬しています。

12. 父親がプロ野球選手のその少年は、野球が上手です。

1. The house (which / that) she bought is very big.

2. The house (which /that) they built is very big.

3. The house (which /that) they built is beautiful.

4. Is the house (which /that) they built beautiful?

5. Is the woman (whom / that) he married beautiful?

6. The woman (whom / that) he married is American.

7. The writer who (that) wrote the novel is American.

8. The man (whom / that) he introduced to me is American.

9. Do they know the man (whom / that) he introduced to me?

10. They don't know the man (whom / that) he introduced to me.

11. They respect the man (whom / that) he introduced to me.

12. The boy whose father is a professional baseball player is good at baseball.

29 関係代名詞—4

DISC 2 TRACK 33

① 海外旅行の好きなその女性は、英語を一生懸命勉強している。

② (彼女の)夢が海外で働くことであるその女性は

③ 　　　　　私が一緒に働いているその女性は

④ 隣に (next door) 住んでいる青年は、とても感じが良いです。

⑤ 彼が私に紹介してくれた青年は、

⑥ 私の娘が付き合っている青年は、　　(付き合う go out with)

⑦ 彼女がペンを借りた少年は、誰ですか？

⑧ メアリーと歩いている少年は、

⑨ 女の子たちが見ている少年は、

⑩ その家を買った男性はとてもお金持ちでした。

⑪ 彼女が恋に落ちた男性は　　　　(恋に落ちる fall in love with)

⑫ 　　　　　　とてもお金持ちでしたか？

1. The woman who (that) likes traveling abroad is studying English hard.

2. The woman whose dream is to work abroad is studying English hard.

3. The woman (whom / that) I work with is studying English hard. / The woman with whom I work is studying English hard.

4. The young man who (that) lives next door is very nice.

5. The young man (whom / that) he introduced to me is very nice.

6. The young man (whom / that) my daughter is going out with is very nice.

7. Who is the boy whose pen she borrowed?

8. Who is the boy who (that) is walking with Mary ?

9. Who is the boy (whom / that) the girls are looking at?

10. The man who (that) bought the house was very rich.

11. The man (whom / that) she fell in love with was very rich.

12. Was the man (whom / that) she fell in love with very rich?

30 関係代名詞—5

DISC 2 TRACK 34

① 私は、彼に私の書いた本を読んで欲しい。

② そのジャーナリストによって書かれた記事を

③ 私がちょうど書き終えた（現在完了）レポートを

④ 自動車事故で怪我をしたその女性は、車を運転することを怖がっています。

⑤ ご両親が自動車事故で亡くなったその女性は

⑥ 怖がっていますか？

⑦ あなたが会いたがっている女性が、明日ここに来るかもしれません。

⑧ あなたに会いたがっている女性が、

⑨ 昨日ここに来ました。

⑩ 車が好きなその男性は、来月新しい車を買う予定です。

⑪ 車が故障したその男性は（故障する break down）

⑫ もう新しい車を買いましたか？

1. I want him to read the book (which / that) I wrote.

2. I want him to read the article which (that) was written by the journalist.

3. I want him to read the report (which / that) I have just finished writing.

4. The woman who (that) was injured in a car accident is afraid of driving.

5. The woman whose parents were killed in a car accident is afraid of driving.

6. Is the woman whose parents were killed in a car accident afraid of driving?

7. The woman (whom / that) you want to meet may (might) come here tomorrow.

8. The woman who (that) wants to meet you may (might) come here tomorrow.

9. The woman who (that) wants to meet you came here yesterday.

10. The man who (that) likes cars is going to buy a new car next month.

11. The man whose car broke down is going to buy a new car next month.

12. Has the man whose car broke down bought a new car yet?

31 原形不定詞─知覚動詞 1

DISC 2 TRACK 35

① 私は彼らが野球をするのを見ました。

② 　　　　　　　家を出発する (leave home) のを

③ 　　　　　　　部屋を掃除するのを

④ 　　　　　　　バスに乗るのを

⑤ 　　　　　　　公園で走るのを

⑥ 彼女は私が英語を話すのを聞いたのですか？

⑦ 　　　　　　　笑うのを

⑧ 　　　　　　　彼と話すのを

⑨ 　　　　　　　ピアノを弾くのを

⑩ 彼らは彼女が部屋に入るのに気づきませんでした。

⑪ 　　　　　　　家を出る

⑫ 　　　　　　　ドアを開ける

1. I saw them play baseball.

2. I saw them leave home.

3. I saw them clean the room.

4. I saw them get on the bus.

5. I saw them run in the park.

6. Did she hear me speak English?

7. Did she hear me laugh?

8. Did she hear me talk to him?

9. Did she hear me play the piano?

10. They didn't notice her go into the room.

11. They didn't notice her leave home.

12. They didn't notice her open the door.

32 原形不定詞―知覚動詞 2

DISC 2 TRACK 36

1. 私は彼女がフランス語を話すのを聞きました。
2. 　　　　　　笑うのを
3. 　　　　　　泣くのを
4. あなたは　　　　　　　　　　　聞きましたか？
5. 　　　　　　トムと話すのを
6. 私たちは　　　　　　　　　見ました。
7. 　　　　　　部屋を掃除するのを
8. 　　　　　　彼がその本を買うのを
9. 彼女は　　　　　　　　　　見ましたか？
10. 　　　　　　教室を出るのを
11. 　　　　　　　　　　　気付きましたか？
12. 私は　　　　　　　　　　気付きませんでした。

1. I heard her speak French.
2. I heard her laugh.
3. I heard her cry.
4. Did you hear her cry?
5. Did you hear her talk to Tom?
6. We saw her talk to Tom.
7. We saw her clean the room.
8. We saw him buy the book.
9. Did she see him buy the book?
10. Did she see him leave the classroom?
11. Did she notice him leave the classroom?
12. I didn't notice him leave the classroom.

33 原形不定詞—使役動詞 1

DISC 2　TRACK 37

① 彼は毎週息子に車を洗わせます。

② 　　　　　ボクシングを練習させます。

③ 　　　　　　　　　　させますか？

④ 　　　　ドイツ語を勉強させますか？

⑤ 私はウェイトレスに（グラス1杯の）水を持ってきてもらった。

⑥ 　　テーブルを片づけてもらった。（テーブルを片付ける clear the table）

⑦ その弁護士は、秘書に手紙をタイプしてもらった。

⑧ 　　　　　　クライアント（client）に電話してもらった。

⑨ 彼女は娘を、友達と映画に行かせてやった。

⑩ 　　　　フランス語のレッスンを受けさせてやった。（レッスンを受ける take lessons）

⑪ 　　　　　　　　受けさせてやるでしょうか？（未来）

⑫ 　　　　　彼女の車を運転させてやるでしょうか？

1. He makes his son wash the car every week.
2. He makes his son practice boxing every week.
3. Does he make his son practice boxing every week?
4. Does he make his son study German every week?
5. I had the waitress bring a glass of water.
6. I had the waitress clear the table.
7. The lawyer had his secretary type the letter.
8. The lawyer had his secretary call the client.
9. She let her daughter go to the movies with her friends.
10. She let her daughter take French lessons.
11. Will she let her daughter take French lessons?
12. Will she let her daughter drive her car?

34 原形不定詞―使役動詞 2

DISC 2 TRACK 38

① 私は彼にこの部屋を掃除させました。

②　　　　　　車を運転させました。

③ あなたは　　　　運転させましたか？

④　　　　　　　運転させたことがありますか？

⑤ 彼女は娘に花に水をやってもらいました。

⑥　　　　皿を洗ってもらいました。

⑦　　　　コーヒーをいれてもらいましたか？

⑧　　　　夕食を作ってもらいましたか？

⑨ 父は僕にそこに行かせてくれました。

⑩　　　　その本を読ませてくれるでしょう。

⑪　　　　その車を運転させてくれます。

⑫　　　　彼の部屋に入らせてくれませんでした。

1. I made him clean this room.

2. I made him drive the car.

3. Did you make him drive the car?

4. Have you ever made him drive the car?

5. She had her daughter water the flowers.

6. She had her daughter wash the dishes.

7. Did she have her daughter make some coffee?

8. Did she have her daughter cook dinner?

9. My father let me go there.

10. My father will let me read the book.

11. My father lets me drive the car.

12. My father didn't let me go into his room.

著者略歴

森沢洋介
もりさわようすけ

1958年神戸生まれ。9歳から30歳まで横浜に暮らす。青山学院大学フランス文学科中退。大学入学後、独自のメソッドで、日本を出ることなく英語を覚える。予備校講師などを経て、1989〜1992年アイルランドのダブリンで旅行業に従事。TOEICスコアは985点。現在千葉浦安で学習法指導を主眼とする、六ツ野英語教室を主宰。
ホームページアドレス　http://homepage3.nifty.com/mutuno/
［著書］英語上達完全マップ
　　　　CD BOOKどんどん話すための瞬間英作文トレーニング
　　　　CD BOOKスラスラ話すための瞬間英作文シャッフルトレーニング
　　　　CD BOOKバンバン話すための瞬間英作文「基本動詞」トレーニング（以上ベレ出版）

◉ CDの内容　◎ DISC1　77分　　DISC2　77分52秒
　　　　　　◎ ナレーション　Edith Kayumi・久末絹代
　　　　　　◎ DISC1とDISC2はビニールケースの中に重なって入っています。

CD BOOK ポンポン話(はな)すための瞬間英作文(しゅんかんえいさくぶん) パターン・プラクティス

2008年 5月25日　初版発行	
2025年 5月27日　第25刷発行	
著者	森沢洋介 もりさわようすけ
カバーデザイン	OAK 小野光一
イラスト・図表	森沢弥生

© Yosuke Morisawa 2008. Printed in Japan

発行者	内田真介
発行・発売	ベレ出版
	〒162-0832 東京都新宿区岩戸町12レベッカビル TEL　03-5225-4790 FAX　03-5225-4795 ホームページ http://www.beret.co.jp/ 振替 00180-7-104058
印刷	三松堂株式会社
製本	根本製本株式会社

落丁本・乱丁本は小社編集部あてにお送りください。送料小社負担にてお取り替えします。

ISBN978-4-86064-193-1 C2082　　　　　　　　編集担当　綿引ゆか

六ツ野英語教室

本書の著者が主宰する学習法指導を主体にする教室です。

🐱 **電話**
0475-77-7123

🐱 **ホームページアドレス**
http://mutuno.sakura.ne.jp/

🐱 **コース案内**

レギュラークラス…週一回の授業をベースに長期的な学習プランで着実に実力をつけます。

トレーニング法セミナー…本書で紹介した「瞬間英作文トレーニング」の他、「音読パッケージ」、「ボキャビル」などトレーニング法のセミナーを定期開催します。

＊〈レギュラークラス〉〈トレーニング法セミナー〉ともにオンラインで受講可能です。